HORRID GO-AHEAD BOY

HORRID GO-AHEAD BOY

A Broadcaster's Life

John Tidmarsh

Book Guild Publishing
Sussex, England

First published in Great Britain in 2010 by
The Book Guild Ltd
Pavilion View
19 New Road
Brighton, BN1 1UF

Typesetting in Garamond by
Keyboard Services, Luton, Bedfordshire

Printed and bound in Great Britain by
CPI Antony Rowe

A catalogue record for this book is available from
The British Library

ISBN 978 1 84624 445 2

Contents

Foreword

About three years after joining the BBC in Bristol as the most junior member of a five man news team, I was sent one evening to the Hippodrome Theatre in the City Centre. Noel Coward was in town to check on the progress of his new musical play, *After the Ball,* inspired by the Oscar Wilde play *Lady Windermere's Fan.* The production was actually being directed not by Coward but by his friend the dancer Robert Helpman. Coward himself had agreed to meet and talk to the local media. All three local papers were there: the *Evening World,* the *Evening Post,* the *Western Daily Press,* where I started my career as a journalist, together with a couple of correspondents based in Bristol to represent Fleet street newspapers in the West Country. The conversation went along in a very amiable manner and, at what I deemed an appropriate moment, I said, 'Mr Coward, I am from the BBC here in Bristol and we would very much like to get an interview with you for our programme *The Week in the West,* which I present. As a matter of fact, I have a recorder outside in my car.'

Coward looked at me with a slight smile and, savouring each word, said, ' "Horrid ... go-ahead ... boy".'

We all laughed. He then went on to say that it would be better if we called him the following day, hinting that they were having a few problems and needed to do a good deal of work on the production before it was fit to wind up a provincial tour and move into London's West End.

Someone else called the theatre the following day as I was busy helping to edit *The Week in the West* and write the script. We never did get the interview, but I had to put up with a good deal of ribbing from friends and colleagues as that 'Horrid Go-ahead boy'. As for

After the Ball it didn't last long in London. To be blunt it was a flop. Helpman in his memoirs writes about Coward and himself growing increasingly desperate over the failure of one particular member of the cast to speak a line that should have provoked laughter.

Sadly I never got another chance to interview Coward. He was not among the many writers, performers, stars of stage and screen, statesmen and politicians, scientists and musicians who came to Bush House in London to talk to me 'live' in *Outlook*, the BBC World Service current affairs and magazine programme that I presented from the moment it was launched in 1966 until I decided to retire in 1997.

Nevertheless, it was not long after meeting Coward that my career really did begin to 'go-ahead'. It was the summer of 1956: the Anglo French invasion of Suez and, subsequently, the Soviet Union and other Warsaw Pact countries sending tanks into Budapest to put down the Hungarian rebellion. BBC News Division was somewhat overstretched and I was asked if I would like to spend a month with the Reporters Unit in London to help out. I must have made a favourable impression because, shortly after returning to Bristol, a message came asking if I would like a permanent job in London. Would I!

Leaving Bristol was going to be a wrench, but the offer was much too good to turn down. It was the beginning of a magic and enormously lucky life that would take me all over the world many many times. First as a special correspondent (France, Algeria, the Middle East, India, the United States, the UN in New York, Africa, Vietnam) and later putting together countless 'on-the-spot' editions of *Outlook* from every Continent, save Antarctica.

In my first ten years on the staff, before I became a Contract freelance for the rest of my career, I spent some time with television News, even as a newsreader. But in those far off years BC (Before Colour) television was not really thought of as a proper job for a serious journalist in news, perhaps with ambitions to find a permanent post abroad. Television reporters were heard, but seen as little as possible – and then only in 'cutaways' used to edit brief interviews. No standing up delivering reports straight to camera. No autocues. Not even in the studio for reading the news. Times have changed, of course. But for me, sitting in a studio in Bush House in the

Strand chatting away to millions of people all round the world, three days a week, has been a huge privilege. Just one of the voices that has helped to sustain what was – I hope still is – the unmatched reputation of the BBC World Service for honest, unbiased reporting of world events, often telling millions of listeners what is actually going on in their own countries, and also giving hope and comfort to many living in dangerous and distressing conditions.

Anthony Grey, locked up in Peking by the Red Guards in the sixties; the Beirut hostages in the eighties – they all became particularly attached to *Outlook* and all came in to thank us personally when they were released. Two of them, Anthony Grey and John McCarthy, actually came to work with us in Bush House. In fact, Tony soon became a Bushman, an extremely useful member of our Bush House cricket team, playing with us in our summer seasons of very attractive fixtures all over southern England.

As for the various reporters and correspondents who were already there when I first joined the BBC I found some of them to be inspirational figures, no-one more so than the man who first managed to draw me into the BBC. That was Frank Gillard, the famous war correspondent, then the Controller of BBC West Region. Frank had a voice and a style that completely captured and held your attention the moment he opened his mouth to speak. In my first year at the BBC in Bristol I not only presented *The Week in the West*, I was also asked to write the one hour review of the *The Year in the West*. The programme was very well received and given excellent ratings, much of it due to my choice of presenter: Frank Gillard! I certainly learnt a great deal in those early years from people like Frank and some of the older correspondents I would meet and often work with when I eventually moved up to News Division in London.

These were men (nearly all men in those days) whom I now think of as colleagues, like Christopher Serpell and Douglas Willis, the two Washington correspondents when I was doing my first assignment abroad at the United Nations in New York. It was there I met Alistair Cooke, an inspirational figure to my generation both as a journalist and a broadcaster. It was partly through that meeting all those years ago that Alistair agreed to give me his only interview when he was celebrating the 50th anniversary of his *Letter from America*.

Doug Willis was also a broadcaster who could immediately hold your attention. I have never forgotten one background despatch he sent when he was eventually moved to a post in Africa and asked to describe the small kingdom within Uganda, based on the North shore of Lake Victoria. A classic example of quickly getting to the point with the basic details, it went like this: 'The place is called Buganda. The people are called the Baganda. Their ruler is called the Kabaka. Their Parliament is called the Lukiiko. The language they speak is Luganda... Also, it rains most afternoons!'

I often wonder why the BBC decided to post Douglas to Africa. Not the wisest place to send someone who was known to have a serious drink problem. Eventually it killed him, but not before we had all responded to his last request: a huge Melton Mowbray pork pie which we had flown out from London. It reached him in time.

There was one other celebrated ex-war correspondent whose company I always enjoyed, Godfrey Talbot. He became the BBC Royal Correspondent and I first came into close contact with him in the late fifties when we travelled around West Africa covering a tour by the Queen and Prince Philip, starting in Ghana when 'Osageyfo the Great Redeemer', otherwise known as Kwame Nkrumah, was still in power. Godfrey had a huge fund of sometimes rather racy, perhaps even rather suspect, stories he was always ready to pass on. Like the fan letter he allegedly received from a woman listener somewhere in France thanking him for helping her with her efforts to learn English. He said it began: 'My dear Mr Talbot, I have long been a fervent of your emissions'!

I suspect it was Godfrey who first told me the story emphasising the need to remember that a 'live' open microphone could inadvertently lead you into saying something you might have put better, something that could be misunderstood. He was often one of a very experienced radio team that did OBs (Outside Broadcasts), going back to the days when voices rather than cameras painted the picture. In September 1955 a number of commentators were in Hastings on the Sussex coast where Winston Churchill went to become another celebrity member of the Fishermen's Charity called The Winkle Club. With him was Field Marshall Montgomery, who was already a member. The Patron of the Club – there were no women members – was

Queen Elizabeth the Queen Mother, who was at the time Warden of the Cinque Ports. The symbol of the Club for ordinary members – of which I am one – is a slightly ornate, polished winkle, the previous occupant having been removed and some red wax put inside to help hold the shell together.

The Queen Mother's was made from solid gold and one just like it was given to Churchill. On the challenge 'Winkle Up' you must produce your Winkle or pay a modest penalty into the charity funds.

The presentation ceremony for Churchill at an end, he and Monty climbed into the back of an open car to drive through cheering crowds lining Hastings seafront. As they passed, someone in the crowd may have shouted out 'Winkle Up'. It was then that one of the commentators suddenly said, 'And now I can see Churchill acknowledging the cheers and he's brandishing his winkle in the air.' (Fortunately, Hastings is the one place where they can't touch you for it!)

I was actually born at almost the same time as the start of broadcasting in Britain. The BBC had been setting itself up, first in Aldwych and then in the Strand. I arrived close by on the opposite side of the Thames in King's College Hospital in Camberwell, eventually to spend nearly fifty years of my life working for the BBC, two-thirds of that time based at Bush House, the home of the world's number one radio station. So how did all that come about? The story begins on August 13th 1928.

1

The Twenties – But Only Just

We called it 'the wireless'. My earliest memories, as with so many children of the thirties, were of getting home from school to have my tea while listening to *Children's Hour*, five o'clock on the National Service with Uncle Mac and Uncle David. We didn't realise at the time that, as one BBC Historian later wrote, '*Children's Hour* provided some of the most intelligent programmes in the whole BBC range with an enthusiastic following among adults as well as children': historical plays by L. du Garde Peach and, my own favourite, Hulme Beaman's classic stories of the adventures in Toytown of Larry the Lamb (played by Derek McCulloch – Uncle Mac) and his friend Denis the Dachshund, who had a very distinctive German accent. (Strange that Denis was such a popular figure when, in our playground 'war games', the Germans were always the enemy). Anyway, the two young animals were often in enough trouble to oblige Ernest the policeman to tell them he was going to have to 'take down their names and addresses'. Of course, nothing more serious ever came of it, much to the disgust of Mister Grouser who was constantly complaining: 'It ought not to be allowed.' More and more my own thoughts these days!

I suppose we would have been thought of as part of what was then a growing middle class. My father was at one time in the Indian Army, an officer in the 32nd Sikhs Regiment based in what is now Pakistan. He remained in India throughout the First World War; very sensible.

He was the eldest of four brothers who all survived that 'war to end all wars'. I often wonder why my father chose to leave the Indian Army. He had risen to the rank of Captain and among his papers I found a document saying that he had passed an exam in basic Hindi. There was also a handy phrase book in which he had written his name and the words: '32 Sikhs, Sialkot, India'. Clearly the book was indispensable for a British officer, keen to enhance his career by improving his language skills. For example, *Modem Colloquial Hindustani* contains several pages about communicating with your Bearer: 'Get the Sweeper'; 'Hold my horse'; 'Bring my boots'; 'Go and get two coolies'. No doubt the latter were needed for more unsavoury duties such as cleaning the 'Thunderbox' – an officer's portable loo!

When my father came home he met my mother in Brighton where she was a leading figure in the local Operatic Society. That is where my story begins. Born in King's College hospital in Camberwell and destined to be an only child, the first home I remember was in New Malden in Surrey – a rather modest flat above the Royal Arsenal Co-operative Society grocery store.

Before long we moved to a new semi-detached house a couple of miles away in Worcester Park. This had a garden front and back, three bedrooms and a garage and cost about £750. We didn't really need the garage as we didn't have a car. My father never got a driving licence. Mother, however, was a bit more ambitious. Towards the end of the thirties she bought and learnt to drive that classic vehicle, an Austin Seven.

Worcester Park liked to think of itself as being much more than a leafy London suburb in Surrey, almost a country village. This was rather emphasised at the Parish school, Malden Parochial, where, to my great disgust, cricket and football gave way to country dancing! So when it came to more manly sports we organised them ourselves out of school hours. I suspect most of us who were primary school children in the thirties knew little or nothing of what was going on outside our own small world. Not like today, when 'The News' is coming out of our radios and television sets morning noon and night – and, on some channels, twenty-four hours a day. *Children's Hour* did do something to widen our horizons, I suppose. The programme had no trouble persuading top speakers to come and talk to us a little about politics, international affairs, natural history, astronomy. Moreover, on occasional visits to the cinema there would always be one of the Newsreels shown before the main feature: Movietone,

Gaumont British, Pathé Gazette, all of them mortally damaged years later by the advent of television.

I don't suppose I paid much attention to them during my earliest visits to our local Odeon to see the curly haired little moppet who was such a star in the thirties, Shirley Temple. And those songs! 'On the good ship lollipop it's a long way to the candy shop . . .' And who could forget the haunting lyrics of 'Animal crackers in my soup, lions and tigers loop the loop . . .'? Only recently I discovered that Shirley, like me, was born in 1928. She is actually four months older and was at one time America's ambassador to Ghana. I wish there had been an opportunity to have her as a 'live' guest on my World Service programme *Outlook*.

I can't remember if *Children's Hour* ever told us about that meeting in Munich between Adolf Hitler and the British Prime Minister, Neville Chamberlain. But I do remember quite clearly the cinema newsreel that showed Chamberlain returning to Heston Airport just outside London to declare to a cheering crowd that there would be 'peace in our time'. Stepping from the aircraft he waved a small piece of paper which, he assured us, bore his signature and that of Adolf Hitler. Actually, the paper may have been blank. At least, that is the story which subsequently gained circulation. If so, it would have been one of the earliest known cases of what we now call 'political spin'. On the credit side is the argument that Chamberlain realised war was probably inevitable and he was only trying to gain time so that Britain would be better prepared.

I had already had my own distant brush with Nazi Germany. All through the middle and late thirties I would spend several weeks of the summer holidays with my grandparents at Bexhill-on-Sea. My grandfather was the manager of Hermitage and Sons, a shop that sold pianos, radios and gramophones. He was also a piano tuner, which gave him the opportunity to travel all over East Sussex and parts of Kent.

Many of the radios in his shop were much grander than the rather basic, bakelite oval-topped box called a Philco which would become more and more the focus of attention in our living room at home. Posher people would have a radiogram, encased in an elegant cabinet that stood on the floor occupying a prominent position, usually to one side of the fireplace.

Before joining my grandfather as the shop closed at the end of the day I could usually look forward to spending a couple of hours on the beach. Grandma would be with me, having taken the precaution to pop into Arscotts the bakers on the way to buy two delicious jam and cream doughnuts, it being well known that small boys playing by the seaside can quickly become absolutely famished. On this particular occasion in, I think, 1936 we were based as usual just in front of that newly completed modernist icon, the De La Warr Pavilion. The tide was out and I was busy creating a sandcastle that would be my own architectural masterpiece. It was what I think of as my Frank Lloyd Wright period. I was dressed in a bathing costume knitted for me by my mother, navy blue with three horizontal yellow stripes across the chest. Crouched over my sandy building site I must have looked from a distance like some terrifying insect, some genetic creation in a laboratory that had gone terribly wrong. Suddenly I became aware that other people on the beach were getting rather excited and, looking up, I saw why.

Close in on the horizon a vast grey sausage was floating by. It was the German airship, the Hindenberg, which would come to a horrible end in the United States the following year, exploding in flames as it attempted to land. Why were they so close to our shore? My guess is they were filming our beaches to plan an invasion later.

I have no doubt that my picture remains somewhere in Germany's military archives. What they made of it, who knows. Did they suspect that Bexhill beach might be infested with a thoroughly dangerous species of insect. All we know is, even in the darkest days of the war, the Nazis never attempted to storm ashore in front of the De La Warr Pavilion.

A childhood in the thirties in our part of south-east England must have been just about as good as you could get – idyllic by today's standards. Close to some gorgeous countryside and not much further to the beaches of the Channel coast for a slightly longer day out: Bexhill, Hastings, Eastbourne and Brighton. We could call on friends and family in most of those places. As for day to day life in Worcester Park I could safely walk to school and back, crossing a field that had not yet been developed for more housing and along a narrow country lane. Mother did get worried, however, if I dawdled a bit on the

4

way home or got briefly diverted by some schoolmates, eventually arriving rather later than she expected. But it was nothing like the anxiety a mother might feel if the same thing happened nowadays. Small wonder so many children are taken to school and collected in the family car, and not allowed to go out on their own at any time.

The thirties were, of course, some fifty or sixty years before schoolchildren needed that vital piece of extra equipment to carry in their back-packs, the mobile phone. (If you have it constantly attached to your ear, can it ultimately damage the brain?) And what about the computer and the internet which the children of today seem to spend so much time ranging over? How many will need glasses while they are still in their teens?

In the thirties we had none of these distractions. Books, jig-saw puzzles, the wireless, out and about in the open air, climbing trees – those were some of our much healthier distractions. There were also some regular rather exciting trips up to London. On the Southern Electric Railway it took around thirty minutes: Motspur Park, Raynes Park, Wimbledon, Clapham Junction and Waterloo. Mother always took me to the very spectacular Ideal Homes Exhibition at Olympia. It is still a hugely popular annual event. The houses that they actually built inside the Exhibition Hall were always the big attraction as they still are today. These London trips often included another great treat; lunch at a Lyons Corner House where the waitresses or 'Nippies' wore those distinctive black and white uniforms with matching head band. No need to show me the menu. I always had the same thing, roast beef.

Back in Worcester Park on a week day you might find us at the local Scout Hut, giving that special salute as Wolf Cubs in response to Akela's call to Dyb Dyb Dyb (Do your best) loudly promising to Dob Dob Dob (Do our best). I eventually became a team leader, a 'Sixer' in the Cubs, thus demonstrating at an early age my innate qualities of leadership!

When it came to books I suppose many children like me started off with something like *Rupert Bear*, moving on to *Winnie-the-Pooh* before tackling something more challenging like *Alice in Wonderland* and identifying almost completely with *Just William* (William Brown). I could always imagine the Brown family living not that far from us in 'leafy Surrey', perhaps in a slightly grander house. The William books by Richmal Crompton, which you can still buy, were very popular with adults as well as children.

It was also a good time for high class comics like *The Magnet*. Billy Bunter (the Owl of the Remove) became one of my favourite characters along with all the others in his form at Greyfriars – the Famous Five: Harry Wharton, Bob Cherry. Frank Nugent, Johnny Bull and Hurree Jamsit Ram Singh (also known as 'Inky' – not very PC by today's ludicrous standards). I wonder if poor old Bunter is still waiting for that postal order which never seemed to come?

I was reading *The Magnet* as I moved closer to my first years in a Grammar School. I had already passed entrance exams for three easily accessible schools. Sadly, what were truly the sunny, carefree years of my childhood were about to come to an end. With the whole family moving over the next five years to three different locations my academic career would suffer greatly.

On 3 September 1939 the whole family was in Bexhill in my grandparent's small bungalow, sitting round the radio at eleven in the morning. Chamberlain, who somehow always contrived to look, dress and sound like a high class Funeral Director, was on the air from 10 Downing Street, his voice very gloomy. His promise after Munich of 'peace in our time' had come apart with Hitler's invasion of Poland. 'We are at War with Germany,' he said, sounding very doom laden.

No sooner had the broadcast ended than the air raid siren started wailing, the rising and falling note that would from that moment on alert us to the approach of enemy aircraft. My grandfather went to the window muttering, 'That didn't take them long.' But it was a false alarm, just a warning to alert those who had not been listening to the radio.

The new school term was about to start. I was in my first pair of long trousers and had a rather smart blazer (navy blue with vertical dark red stripes) ready for my first term at Tiffins Boys' School in Kingston-upon-Thames, my first choice from among those three grammar schools that had offered me a place. Was I quite bright in those days? Then came the news that school had been postponed until further notice. War couldn't be that bad after all! Certainly not for us eleven-year-old schoolboys, though no doubt my parents were already wondering if it would all be over before I was called up for active service. It would turn out to be a close call.

At first in that autumn of 1939 nothing much seemed to have changed. My father went off each week-day morning on the 8.15 from Worcester Park to Waterloo to get to his office in Holborn. After leaving the Indian Army he had become a civil servant and was now working for the Inland Revenue. I was soon proudly making my way to school by bus from Worcester Park to New Malden, then on one of those lovely old double-decker red trolley buses from New Malden to the gates of the school. There was no 'school run' in those days of private family cars, often carrying only one child, causing chaos in the morning 'rush hour'. There was no 'rush hour' on the roads. Most people commuted to work by bus and trolley bus or the Southern Electric railway to London.

Some of us had fairly modest cars, like our Austin Seven, but they often remained in the garage until a sunny week-end would encourage a little 'run out', perhaps to somewhere in the country. Wartime petrol rationing soon put a stop to that. And certainly the authentic country was now much further from London than it used to be. The twenties and thirties had seen huge housing developments of detached and semi-detached homes, often with an integral garage and gardens front and rear, on the market for less than a thousand pounds, just like ours. They had sprung up in all the home counties, encircling London. And into these homes moved people like us.

Although I felt so little had changed, that autumn was already very different for hundreds of children of my age, and very much younger, who were still living in the middle of London and thought to be in mortal danger of a visit from the *Luftwaffe*. The East End and the Docklands were certain to be a primary target for the bombers. London's main line railway stations witnessed many tearful scenes as hundreds of carefully labelled youngsters, each carrying a gas mask around the neck in a small brown cardboard box, were bundled onto trains to be billeted for the time being on foster parents somewhere safer. Before long I too would be an evacuee, although at first we were moved to distant parts as a family.

I spent just one term at Tiffins School before Father told us that we were all three of us going to Llandudno in North Wales. Where?

Never heard of it. I had never been further North than Regent's Park
Zoo in London. But, like the young evacuees, the country's civil
servants also had to be moved to places of greater safety outside
London in order to carry out the business of Government. I don't
doubt keeping the tax collectors safe was seen as a priority. In due
course we were at Euston Station about to embark on a journey that
would take five or six hours. The sad evacuees were no longer there
but the station was teeming with service men and women in uniform:
soldiers, sailors, airmen, most of them not sure where their own
journey would end. And even if they knew they couldn't tell any of
the tearful relatives who had come to see them off and wonder when
(or even if) they would meet again. Posters everywhere implored us
to keep what we knew (or thought we knew) to ourselves because
'Careless Talk Costs Lives'.

The lovely Vera Lynn (later Dame Vera) – another of my 'live'
studio guests years later in *Outlook* – did her best during the war to
cheer everyone up with the much loved song, 'We'll meet again, don't
know where don't know when...'. Optimistic, but at the same time
touching the uncertainty and anxiety of the times. I have one other
vivid memory of Euston: that fragrant smell of coal smoke and steam
that has long since disappeared from our stations – as, indeed, have
the great steam engines that hauled the exciting express trains of the
day.

It was all aboard the Glasgow Express – change at Crewe – for
Llandudno. The train was absolutely packed, many passengers jammed
together in the corridors. Even if you had a window seat it was not
that easy to enjoy the passing scenery. All the windows were covered
in netting to stop glass splinters flying about if we were bombed. In
any case, you had largely to guess where you were. Station names
had been removed to confuse the enemy, but advertisements on the
platform remained, so any spies recently parachuted into Britain, or
Fifth Columnists, travelling by train would keep finding themselves
at places called 'Bovril' or 'Horlicks'.

And what did they make of that well-known holiday resort, 'Virol
– Anaemic Girls Need It'?

I can't remember if they took down the station names in North
Wales but, on reflection, it probably wasn't necessary. Imagine for a

moment some unfortunate enemy agent parachuting into North Wales, many miles from the agreed dropping zone in England, where his contacts are still anxiously awaiting his arrival. He has a problem. First of all he must find out exactly where he is. One answer is to look for a railway line and follow it until he arrives at a station. But when he eventually does find a small station what does it say on a sign that runs virtually the length of the entire platform?

LLANFAIRPWLLGWYNGYLLGOGERYCHWYRNDROBWL LLLANTYSILIOGOGOGOCH

On the island of Anglesey it is the longest place name in Wales – or anywhere else as far as I know. If he knew where he was our unhappy agent could try to escape across the Irish Sea to neutral Eire, as it was then called. Or he could give himself up and offer to become a double agent. Failing that the 'suicide pill' was probably the best way out.

Although I was excused Welsh lessons at my next grammar school – the John Bright County in Llandudno – I did learn to say the longest place name. It has been for many years one of my party pieces. I still have very happy memories of the year or so we spent in Llandudno. From a suburb in Surrey to an attractive seaside resort was not a bad exchange. Some of my school friends were also evacuees from the south and, when we were not on the seafront, we enjoyed 'mountaineering' as we clambered up and down the Great Orme, the large headland at the western end of the town.

Our home in Llandudno was the top floor of a large boarding house: two bedrooms and a bathroom which we shared with the family on the floor below, mother and father and two daughters, refugees from the Netherlands. It was, no doubt, the best the Inland Revenue could do for us.

We were soon into the period when Britain, standing alone, was being pounded every night by the *Luftwaffe*. Every time we heard the wailing rise and fall of the air raid siren a dramatic little scene took place just inside the front door of our boarding house. Mrs Jones, our landlady, would frantically open the cupboard under the stairs, throw out some of the contents into the hallway, and shut herself inside until she was convinced the danger was past. The bombers were usually on their way to Liverpool. We were too far away to hear the bombs exploding but we could often see on the horizon the night sky lit up by the flames below. Mrs Jones seemed convinced that Adolf bore some personal animosity towards Llandudno. We did have one bomb dropped nearby. It may have been meant for a train, the Holyhead Express, but it fell in open country, destroying the only house for miles around and killing the inhabitants.

We were shown that the *Luftwaffe* had also paid a price when, one morning walking along the sea front, we came across a *Heinkel* bomber, shot down and put on display, presumably to raise morale. There was also further evidence of the activities of our brave lads in the RAF when a Spitfire made a successful crash landing on the school playing fields. Strange to think that the pilot was probably no more than seven years older than us twelve-year-olds in the first form.

I don't know why the Inland Revenue couldn't decide where it was safest for my father to be playing his part in keeping watch over the Nation's finances, but, some months before my thirteenth birthday, we were on our way again. It was back to the South and the town of Reading in Berkshire, forty miles west of London.

This time we were allocated a whole house to ourselves, a terraced property in one of the least attractive quarters just off Southampton Street. It had no electricity, only gaslight, no bathroom, and the lavatory was in the yard outside the backdoor – not a place to linger in mid-winter. Bathing took place in a tin bath in the scullery, which had to be filled up with kettles of hot water boiled on the stove. That is how we all managed to remain reasonably fragrant. In any case, even if you had a proper bathroom and bath you were supposed to fill it with only a few of inches of water – another form of wartime rationing. The most immediate problem though was the precious wireless. The six o'clock news could not be missed. To keep it going we had to fix our faithful Philco to a small accumulator. We had three of them altogether, which had to be re-charged at a local shop. At least one was always on stand-by for the moment when the one in use began to fade.

It was not exactly the sort of home in which you would expect to find a former Captain in the Indian Army and his family, but it was certainly better than sharing yet another boarding house. I have to admit we were so much better off than thousands of families all over Britain as the *Luftwaffe* pounded London and other major cities night after night.

This was the height of the Blitz, a time when so many families returning from a night in the nearest air raid shelter would come out to find their homes reduced to a pile of rubble. Official statistics say sixty-thousand civilians were killed in the Second World War. Did we have any idea of the extent of the day to day casualties? I suspect not. News, like almost everything else, was carefully rationed.

Speaking of rationing, when you look back and see how severe it was in those days you may wonder how we survived. Any complaints about shortages ... 'sorry we've run out' ... invited the familiar rebuke: 'Don't you know there's a war on.' In fact, though the shortages meant we ate fewer eggs and less meat, fat and sugar I suspect we wartime children grew up on a much healthier diet than children today. As far as I remember there was no-one at any of my schools we called 'Fatty' or 'Bunter'.

My third grammar school in less than two years was Archbishop Tenison's. As it was located opposite the Oval cricket ground in south London, the whole school had been evacuated to Reading and was sharing facilities with Reading School. The junior forms of which I became a member, lived rather grandly. We were taught in a large country house at Earley on the outskirts of Reading. South Lodge stood in several acres of delightful wooded grounds with its own huge lake, much enjoyed by us in the summer months. To my absolute disgust, South Lodge is now a vast post-war housing estate and the very room where I was taught Maths, English, Geography, and History, and struggled to learn Latin is now furnished as a bar. The lovely house has been turned into a pub.

While I took the trolley bus to school each day, my mother, an officer in the Red Cross, later promoted to Commandant, worked in a factory, running a clinic. My father spent many of his off duty hours with the Home Guard. He would later be manning an anti-aircraft battery. 'Dad's Army', as they came to be called, were now much better equipped than in those earliest days when, as the LDV (Local Defence Volunteers), they were often jokingly referred to as

'Look, Duck and Vanish'. Joking apart, withdrawing would have been a sensible manoeuvre if they had sighted the enemy in those early days as, at the start, they didn't even have rifles with which to defend themselves.

Before long I became a genuine evacuee, like most of my school mates. Father was moved yet again, this time to Bristol to work for the War Damage Commission. I was sent to live with a family at Woodley, within walking distance of school, another house that had only gaslight, though I greatly enjoyed going to bed by candlelight. In the summer term that year I reached my peak as an athlete. To prove it I still have a certificate which says it was awarded in time of war in place of a cup to: 'John Tidmarsh, First in the High Jump (Under Thirteen)'. Cricket and soccer were my preferred sports. My other very happy memory of my time at Tenison's was the summer we went camping at a school in nearby Hungerford to help bring in the harvest. My rôle was rather modest: leading a horse and cart out to the fields to be loaded up and then taken to where the grain was to be stored.

In the long summer holiday I went, of course, to be with my parents in Bristol. This time we had a splendid old house in Henleaze Gardens, one of the most superior parts of the city. My parents were naturally reluctant to let their only child go back to being an evacuee and, I think rather reluctantly since I had enjoyed the freedom, I decided to stay. In any case they had already found me a place at my fourth Grammar School – Cotham Grammar.

Academically, I was by this time beginning to lose the plot. English and History were not a problem but Maths was disastrous. Ms Bailey, our rather deaf Latin mistress, obviously thought I was never going to be a classical scholar, so I was moved from form 4a to 4c where the curriculum included woodwork and metalwork. Clearly they felt the best I could hope for in the future was a job as some sort of workman: plumber, perhaps, or bricklayer – or, if I was very lucky, a career in the Services. At the end of the summer term in 1944, total disaster. Looking for my name at the University building at the top of Park Street to see if I had passed my school certificate, I saw to my horror that it was missing. I may have done well in several subjects, but not, I suspect in Maths, which would mean automatic failure. What now? End it all with a leap off the famous Clifton Suspension Bridge? Run away to sea? In truth, I cannot remember feeling greatly agitated, and the next few months in Form 5x went wonderfully well.

Along with several others I took a crash course to get the Oxford School certificate in the examinations held just before Christmas. I somehow improved my Maths, and two delightful ladies who lived next door to us in Henleaze Gardens helped me with my French. As a result, I finally achieved a decent level of Credits and Passes. So ended my academic career.

Looking back, if anything saved me it was history and cricket. I discovered one Games afternoon in a practice match that I could be a rather fearsome fast bowler. Twice in one over I clean bowled the Second Eleven captain. I was picked immediately for the next match at Weston Super Mare where I took six for twenty-four. The link between cricket and history was Bert Crewe, our history master. He was a member of the Gloucestershire County Cricket Club and I played for his team in one or two limited over evening matches on the County Ground. Not for the County, of course; it was Bert Crewe's Eleven.

Three Cotham boys of my time did go on to play not only for the County but also for England: the bowlers David Allen and John Mortimore and, the last person to be capped for England in both Cricket and Soccer, Arthur Milton. I was briefly in the same form as Arthur and met him again years later when, his sporting career over, he was working as a postman. He was evidently a very happy man. I was also at his Memorial Service in 2007 when the Church at Westbury-on-Trym was absolutely packed with those of us who knew him, not only as a great sportsman but as a most amiable and modest person with a great sense of humour.

But back to dear old Bert. He is the one who helped to launch me on a career that was to last more than fifty years. Good heavens! Can it really be that long? Bert heard me saying that I was keen to try journalism and, apparently, he had some very good contacts on the local morning newspaper, the *Western Daily Press*. He somehow persuaded them to take me on as a junior reporter. Wartime meant that some of the senior staff were away in the Forces and they knew that I also would be called up in about eighteen months' time. I was sixteen and a half, with ambitions to join the RAF. In the meantime I would receive the princely sum of £1.10s a week, plus five shillings for what they called 'In town expenses'. That was to cover, no questions asked, such things as bus fares. I can't remember how much it cost to take a bus to, for example, Staple Hill Police Court on the outskirts of the city or, a little further, to Chipping Sodbury Council – a few pennies, no more. So I suspect I may have made a slight profit on my 'in town expenses'.

For most of the time I was not much more than an office boy: first to arrive in the Reporters' Room in the morning to sit at the telephone switchboard and never being despatched much further than the Coroner's Court, close to the city centre. It was a few lines from there that saw me appear in print for the first time: 'At Bristol Coroner's Court yesterday a verdict of accidental death was recorded on...'. I can't remember the poor fellow's name, but he had been 'in collision with' (as we carefully said in those days) a lorry while cycling along Brislington Road.

Bristol during the war was a very dull place. The shopping centre had been destroyed in a raid just before we arrived (good timing again) and on Sundays, under the stifling influence of church and chapel, the whole city seemed to close down. Not much for us lads to do – my old schoolfriends, Peter, Albert, Brian and me – but kick a football on Durdham Downs. A popular rendezvous was the Milk Bar at the top of Blackboy Hill, though we did 'go clubbing' once a week. I refer to the local youth club in the church hall!

As a junior reporter I never managed to get more than a few lines into the *Western Daily Press*, not least because it was such a sparse newspaper in those wartime days. Newsprint was also in short supply so the paper had only four pages. A broadsheet like *The Times*, it had small ads all over the front page, news and features on pages two and three, and sport on page four, the back page. I was occasionally given tickets to see the new production at the local Rep., the Rapier Players, and this opened the way for a delightful friendship with a girl called Denise Carpenter, who was always happy to accompany me.

Denise later became a Bluebell Girl at the *Folies Bergère* in Paris.

I was actually with her the night Bristol went completely barmy. VE Night, the end of the war in Europe. Vast crowds, singing and dancing, completely blocked the city centre and I have a cherished memory of dancing the polka with Denise most of the way up Park Street, the steep hill that leads from the centre to the university tower at the top. How on earth did I lose touch with Denise? I suppose it was when the time came for me to serve King and Country and I was posted to the Far East.

With National Service looming I had already been up to RAF Hornchurch in Essex, just outside London, to appear before an Air Crew Selection Board. I still like to think that the fact I was selected had little to do with the coincidence of a distant relative being chairman of the board! It was during these two or three days in London that I had a first hand, close-up view of Hitler's last desperate effort to avoid total defeat: the V1 flying bombs, or 'Doodlebugs' as they were nicknamed. Sounding rather like a noisy motor cycle, you could hear one coming from some way off. When you looked up and saw one almost overhead you quietly muttered, 'Go on ... go on!' – to somewhere else. The moment the engine stopped it would plunge straight down to the ground. One fell not more than eighty yards from our house in Worcester Park. Worse was to come when the V2 rocket arrived. This gave no warning. There was just a sudden huge explosion.

I was about to celebrate my seventeenth birthday when I had to register for National Service. I was awoken one night by a tremendous noise coming from a house on the other side of Henleaze Gardens occupied by Service people, mainly army personnel. Jubilant celebrations were under way. The War was over. Japan had surrendered or, as the Emperor himself put it, '... decided to stop fighting as the War was not going as Japan would have wished.' Strange to think that the man who brought the Second World War to an end so dramatically, so historically, by taking the decision to drop the atomic bomb on Hiroshima and then Nagasaki, had known absolutely nothing of the top secret plans to develop the weapon – the Manhattan Project. It was evidently felt that, as Roosevelt's Vice-President, Harry Truman had no need to know. It was only when he took over the White House on the death of FDR that someone had to let him in on the secret. I have always felt a tremendous admiration for Truman, and not just because the decision to drop the bomb brought the war to an unexpected end, probably saving tens of thousands of lives, maybe mine amongst them. It was also his determination to do a job he had never expected and, initially, felt none too confident about his ability to do. At the outset many looked on this once bankrupt draper from the small town of Independence, Missouri, in middle America as a huge letdown after FDR. Once the euphoria at the end of the war had faded Truman found himself struggling at home in the US with severe problems: shortages, rising prices, one strike after another. 'Peace is hell,' he once said.

His efforts to introduce a higher minimum wage, health insurance for all Americans, civil rights, were all rejected by an alliance in Congress of Republicans and conservative Southern Democrats. But he did succeed in desegregating the armed forces. And yet, in 1948, when he went for a second term in the White House he brought off what has rightly been called the biggest upset in American political history. Truman was about the only person who thought he could beat the suave, self-confident Republican candidate, Thomas Dewey, Governor of New York. Even his wife, Bess Truman, had her doubts. But on the morning after the election there was a glorious picture of a broadly smiling Truman holding up the front page of the *Chicago Daily Tribune* with its banner headline falsely declaring 'Dewey Beats Truman'.

Only a few years ago – this time on American Television – we have seen other examples of the way the headlong rush to be first with the news can subsequently provoke a great deal of derisive laughter if it is wrong. I see it also as a victory for the American people, rejecting what all those experts and analysts had told them they were going to do. More about Truman later from the exclusive interview I did with Alistair Cooke.

Exactly a year after the War ended I said goodbye to the *Western Daily Press* and went to Warrington in Lancashire and nearby RAF Padgate. Here I collected an RAF uniform and some other essential kit and became overnight an AC2 (Aircraftsman Second Class), otherwise known as an 'Erk'. I was then posted south to RAF Yatesbury in Wiltshire, just outside Chippenham, for eight weeks of initial training, or 'square bashing'. We spent hours marching up and down the parade ground, practising basic rifle drill, occasionally fixing our bayonets on the front of very elderly Lee Enfield rifles and then rushing forward to impale an imaginary enemy in the form of a sack of hay hanging from a pole. Corporal Jones in the wonderful *Dad's Army* may have insisted 'they don't like it up 'em', but none of it seemed to have much relevance to being an aircraftsman. Surely we don't do rifles, do we? That's for the RAF Regiment.

It was one of the worst winters since the war, so when the weather was too bad for such larks we were put on 'fatigues' in the cookhouse peeling potatoes, or made ourselves busy polishing our buttons and our boots ready for the CO's inspection. Another very heavy snow storm in that bitterly cold winter forced our distraught Flt Sgt to tell us that the final Passing Out Parade was cancelled. He added that it was just as well as we were the 'worst bloody shower to join His Majesty's Air Force since Pontius was a pilot'. I wonder if this awful joke, and others nearly as bad, still circulate in the RAF of today?

Basic training over I was about to get my very first experience of speaking into a live microphone. From Yatesbury I was posted to RAF St Athan, near Bridgend in South Wales, then one of the largest RAF stations in Britain. My 'trade', should I decide to do what was likely to be no more than two years' National Service, would be to work as an RT/Op. (radio operator). If I opted for aircrew training I was told I would have to sign on for five years. The War was now over and 'civvy street' was beginning to look more attractive – the possibility of winding up one day in Fleet Street even more so. Flying? Or back to newspaper journalism? It was decision time. With some reluctance I set aside the long held vision of myself as Sqn Ldr Tidmarsh, the epitome of a daring fighter ace, large silk polka-dot kerchief casually knotted at the throat. Just as well, perhaps. I may have turned out to be much closer to Pilot Officer Prune, the casualty prone cartoon figure featured on those cautionary RAF posters illustrating how to avoid basic errors. Like not touching down on the runway *before* lowering the undercarriage!

For the next few weeks, I became the junior member of the team operating the St Athan control tower. ('Fox-Baker this is St Athan tower. You are clear to join our circuit at one thousand feet. Runway three zero. Call me down wind. Over...'; to which the reply was: 'Roger, tower. Runway three zero.') Yes, as I learnt when I was then posted to the Signals Training Unit at RAF Cranwell, a new and essential vocabulary was part of the course.

It was at Cranwell that I knew I had taken the right decision. The moment the course was over I was told, along with most of the others in my class, that I was being posted to Singapore. What an adventure! I don't think anyone in our group had ever been abroad – not even across The Channel to France. The nearest I had come to it was Bexhill-on-Sea.

After a brief embarkation leave, and having been kitted out for The Tropics (mosquito net included), I found myself one late summer evening on the stern of the troopship *Empress of Scotland* watching the skyline of Liverpool slowly fading from view. (Incidentally, all the deck maps on the *Empress of Scotland* still bore the ship's original name: *Empress of Japan*!)

She had obviously been a well equipped, even luxurious, liner in her day, sailing back and forth to the Empire and colonies and, no doubt, carrying more than a few young ladies, known as 'The Fishing Fleet', all hoping to land a husband. Our quarters were somewhat less than luxurious: below decks, at the level of the cargo holds, and furnished with two tier and three tier bunks – not unlike a German PoW Camp. Not that we complained. We remained cheerful and good humoured, spending as much time as possible on the third class deck and occasionally sleeping there. Tropic nights under the stars.

Within three weeks we had slipped through the Mediterranean and down the Suez Canal, and were contemplating the awesome spectacle of a violent tropical thunderstorm along the coast of Indonesia: Bible black skies (as Dylan Thomas would have called them) lit up every few moments with searing bursts of lightning.

Next morning we had docked at Singapore. Instead of going to a transit camp I was posted immediately to RAF Seletar in the north of the island, overlooking the Straits of Johore. On my arrival in the Signals Section I was greeted like some visitor from outer space. New arrivals straight from home were often called 'Moon Men' and I was the first RT/Op. they had seen for ages. Some time after the end of the War in the Far East impatience had come very close to rebellion among some RAF personnel who felt they were long overdue for demob. Indeed, the growing anger at the delay in getting back to 'civvy street' and finding a job before all the best had been taken by service people already being demobbed in Europe had exploded well beyond Singapore and Malaya.

For me, though, it was the start of an enormously enjoyable year. I was to operate the VHF/DF (Direction Finder) which was housed in a fifteen hundredweight truck parked out on the airfield. Inside the truck were a transmitter and a receiver and a small wheel to turn the aerial protruding through the roof, thus allowing it to revolve through 360 degrees.

It was, as it sounds, rather a basic piece of gear. When one of our brave lads couldn't decide whether he was on the west coast or the east coast of Malaya (or possibly somewhere in between) he would call up for a bearing. I would then instruct him to transmit for ten seconds or so while I turned the wheel and the aerial until his voice faded. I then pressed a button and, if his voice returned, read a bearing from the calibrated scale which turned with the wheel. 'Baker Charlie, this is Seletar Homer. Steer 143. I say again, steer 143. ... 'Roger Seletar. 143. Thank you.'

I said the equipment was a bit basic. If something had upset it then it was perfectly possible to give poor old Baker Charlie and others like him a reciprocal bearing which, instead of bringing them safely back to base, would send them off in exactly the opposite direction. In that case, at least you could be sure they would never come back to complain! Actually, in order to check the accuracy of the original bearing, they were asked to call again a few moments later before they could get out of range.

Someone had to be out on the VHF/DF van all night and sleep there in order to go into action in any emergency and to cover the occasional night flying exercises. My opposite number didn't really fancy it, so I did two nights in a row, mainly sleeping peacefully on a mattress on the floor of the truck, followed by one long day. This gave me plenty of time off duty, allowing for an early game of tennis before the sun got too hot, followed by several hours larking about in the camp swimming pool.

As shift workers we could eat at any time. A late lunch was followed by a bit of a 'zizz' in the afternoon before getting ready to play in the Signals soccer team. Then came a visit to the Malcolm Club for a glass or two of Tiger, or maybe the camp cinema where the programme changed two or three times each week. It was all go!

Occasionally, we took a day off in Singapore, transported there and back in the 'bus service' run by our own trucks. On the first occasion we were allowed into Singapore the Signals Officer gave us young lads of eighteen or nineteen some fatherly advice.

'Some of you,' he said, 'are going into Singapore just to have a good time. Some of you may be going with other intentions. By that I mean ... wanting to get your ends away. I can tell you now, lads,' he continued with some emphasis, 'I can tell you now ... it's a bit dicey.'

In spite of this good advice we did have one corporal who lost his stripes more than once after 'picking up a dose', as it was called. Anyone fearing they may have contracted some sort of infection, even during protected sex, had a later opportunity to take a further precaution. Just inside the main gate at Seletar was a place called the ET Room. It was not the place where we kept captured Aliens from another planet – ET stood for Early Treatment. Never having paid it a visit myself (honestly), I always assumed it involved something fairly basic – not much more than a bit of ointment you dabbed on the endangered articles.

In spite of scrupulous standards of hygiene and cleanliness and the liberal application of Johnson's Baby Powder in susceptible areas, there was one infection that attacked even the innocent. Septic Prickly Heat could occasionally come up on the inside leg, close to the groin. The treatment for this was to visit the MO who would paint the area with a rather astringent mixture called Gentian Violet.

You could always tell when some poor fellow was returning to E-Block, where we lived, after some of the treatment had been inadvertently brushed against his testicles. Much to our amusement he would seem to be hopping about from one leg to the other in a useless effort to shake off the acute stinging sensation. Relief would only come when he reached the sanctuary of the showers and, I assume, applied cold water to the distressed area – though that might have made it worse.

Christmas 1947 at RAF Seletar was for most of us in my group the first we had ever spent away from family and friends. I seem to remember – though rather vaguely as a good deal of Tiger beer had been taken on board – that we had quite a good time: an excellent Christmas lunch in the airmen's mess with, in keeping with tradition, the officers waiting on us. Then it was on into the New Year, 1948, knowing that, in about eight months' time, we would be on our way home to be demobbed, our two years' National Service at an end.

Little did we know then how close we came to staying a good deal longer. Communist guerrillas or bandits were becoming increasingly active in Malaya. It was the start of what came to be known as 'The Emergency', the attempt by the Communists, led by a man called Chin Peng, to turn Malaya and Singapore into a Communist state. Instead, with the Communists finally routed, it led to the independence of the country we now know as Malaysia, initially joined with Singapore until the island chose to break away to enjoy its own complete independence.

Blissfully unaware that things were becoming rather serious, a group of us decided to take local leave on the gorgeous island of Penang. In the place where there are now so many tourist hotels we had our own private and almost deserted beach. It was our own exclusive holiday camp run by the Malcolm Clubs, that splendid institution first set up during the Second World War by Air Chief Marshal Lord Teddar as a place where ordinary airmen could enjoy something similar to an Officers' Club. The first of them opened in Algiers in 1943 and was named after an heroic Bomber Squadron pilot, Wing Cdr Malcolm, the first Air Force VC in the North Africa campaign, who had been killed in December the year before. I remember the ladies who ran the Club in Penang with some affection; they were very jolly and sporty in the way they looked after us and tried to make sure we had a good time. Nowadays I could imagine them posing in the nude for a very tasteful Malcolm Club calendar as the redoubtable ladies of the WI have done.

What with swimming, sunbathing (gaining a very good tan for when we got home was essential) and barbecues on the beach in the evening, our week went by all too quickly. We also made one or two night time visits into Georgetown where a place called The City Lights was a popular venue. Here you could buy several tickets for a dollar or two to take the floor with any one of a number of available young ladies known as 'taxi dancers'. No other services were available, though one of our lads became so enamoured with the girl he danced with several times, he later went AWOL just to be with her.

The manner of our return to Singapore was, as I now realise, indicative that 'The Emergency' was gathering momentum. We had travelled to Penang from Singapore by train, each of us made to carry a rifle as the railway was, as we learnt later, a popular target for the guerrillas. Now we were told we would be flying back to Singapore from RAF Butterworth, on the mainland opposite Penang island.

Back at Seletar as the weeks ticked by it was time to pay further visits to the local village tailor, Abdul Latheef. At home in Britain clothing was rationed, so we needed some new shirts in a smart fabric called 'sharkskin', some well tailored trousers for winter and summer and, perhaps, an elegant sports jacket. The prices at dear old Abdul's were very reasonable.

Then, suddenly, our demob. number had come up. I think mine was 76. I collected my pay book from the Signals Officer as I said goodbye. I had been acting as his secretary in the last few weeks in order to exercise my shorthand ready for being back at the *Western Daily Press*. In a brief summary of my year at Seletar he had written in the book that I was 'a very capable and reliable airman able to use his own initiative'. Unfortunately, he had misspelled 'initiative', making it 'inititive'. Never mind; the thought was there. Soon we were singing a song we had long rehearsed: 'The best sight in Singapore without any doubt is from the aft end of a troopship that's on its way out.'

Whatever I felt at the time I must admit that today I have a great nostalgia for 'Singers' and often stop off there on my annual visits to Australia to avoid the British winter. The troopship *Devonshire* was a distinct improvement on the *Empress of Scotland*. Our quarters were no longer way down below, alongside the cargo holds. This time we slept in hammocks on our own mess deck, where we also ate. Portholes gave not only a view but extra ventilation. What luxury!

I have just one special memory of that four week journey home. We were anchored to take on supplies at Port Said at the top of the Suez Canal. Just across the water from us was a French troopship.

We entertained each other in turn with a bit of an impromptu sing-song. I often wonder how many of the lads on that French ship finally made it home.

They were on their way to Vietnam, which ended in disaster for the French at Dien Bien Phu. Some seventeen years later I would also be in Vietnam as a correspondent for the BBC.

Whenever I remember that moment in Port Said it reminds me how lucky my age group was to do our National Service when we did. The Second World War had been over for a year, 'The Emergency' in Malaya was only just beginning to gather momentum, the Korean War had not yet started. We did our National Service in what were virtually the two most peaceful years of the second half of the twentieth century. Between 1948 and 1960 one and a half million eighteen-year-olds were called up for National Service; one in twelve of them went to operational areas. According to official figures, four hundred were killed in Malaya, Korea, Cyprus, Suez, Kenya and Aden.

The final leg of our journey home in the autumn of 1948 took us from Port Said on a pleasant cruise along the Mediterranean, saluting Gibraltar as we turned into the Atlantic and having a rather bumpy ride across the Bay of Biscay. One morning several absentees from our mess table allowed me to enjoy not one, but three, kippers – my favourite breakfast. Finally, we were back where we started, the Port of Liverpool.

There followed two days at RAF Kirkham to be formally demobbed and kitted out by a grateful nation for life in civvy street. My demob clothes included a navy blue, pin stripe suit and a beige raincoat of the type worn by all the best private eyes in those glorious films *noir* of the period. One of my favourites is *Farewell My Lovely*, starring Dick Powell – unmissable.

I enjoyed several weeks' paid leave – then it was back to work at the *Western Daily Press* – blue suit, raincoat and highly polished black shoes. I am not sure the paper was delighted to see me again, but they were obliged by law to give me back my civvy job after I had served King and Country.

Bristol was still a rather dull grey place in the late forties and early fifties, compared with our life in Singapore. Food and clothing were rationed, café life was barely visible, and an acute shortage of housing had driven many families to move in as squatters where former army camps had been left empty.

The broadsheet *WDP* was still a rather drab, unspectacular version of the journalistic arts. Small ads remaining on the front page and there were no bylincs apart from Man 'o Mendip, the agricultural correspondent, AGP, the elderly chief reporter Archie Powell with his 'Notes of the Day', and LRB, the music critic. Leo Reid Baker was, in fact, the owner of the paper. He played the oboe and was often pressed in to service in the wind section of a visiting orchestra.

As a general reporter I had more than my fair share of the Magistrates' Court (any defendant coming from Knowle West and described as a 'general dealer' was almost certainly guilty), the Coroner's Court, Staple Hill Court, Sodbury District Council and, from time to time, the Divorce Court.

My attendance at this last was a completely futile exercise as the evidence in a defended divorce could not be reported, only the outcome. It did, however, provide some unusual insights into the lives of some Bristolians. I remember the petitioner who said that he came home one evening and found his wife in bed with another man. Sounding absolutely scandalised the judge asked him what he did next.

'My Lord,' he replied rather sheepishly, 'I said "Good evening".'

Usually on a Monday there were two tickets for the latest production at the Little Theatre by the local Repertory Company, the Rapier Players. From time to time there were also tickets for a new show at The Hippodrome. Nothing came from the Empire Music Hall in Old Market. They knew that the *WDP* would never countenance a review of shows like *Strip, Strip, Hooray*.

Outside working hours a popular watering hole for both the *WDP* and the *Evening World* was the pub called The Artichoke on Christmas Steps. I was very friendly with several people from the *Evening World*, not least Ted Trimmer, the brother of the film star Deborah Kerr. The sports editor, George Baker, and the sports reporter, Peter Barnes, recruited me to play for them in their limited over evening cricket matches in some of the most delightful places in south Gloucestershire and north Somerset. My addiction to sport eventually opened the way for me to a career in broadcasting.

For the *WDP* I became the reporter who followed the fortunes every Saturday of Bristol Rovers. In those days 'The Pirates' (their nickname) were thought unlikely to plunder anything except relegation and were very much the inferior of the other Bristol team, Bristol City. Then, all of a sudden, things changed. Bert Tann, a former Charlton player and one of the most amiable and likeable managers the game has ever seen, took them to heights they had never known before. Once they came within an inch of reaching the semi-finals of the FA Cup.

Playing Newcastle United at St James' Park, Newcastle, the centre forward, Vic Lambden, struck the foot of the post of the Newcastle goal barely seconds before the end of the game. It finished as a draw, but Rovers lost the replay in Bristol.

Such was the interest in soccer in those days that the fairly new Hospital Broadcasting system decided to organise commentaries from Saturday home games. I was asked to be one of the commentators. Did I model myself on Raymond Glendenning, the great BBC commentator of the time? I think I was probably a bit more excitable. Anyway, after one very lively game, some kind person with contacts in BBC West Region in Whiteladies Road put it about that I might make a good broadcaster. To my great surprise, the BBC got in touch with me. Initially this created a problem. For some reason the *WDP* frowned on any of its staff working elsewhere, particularly 'the Beeb'. So when I was asked to do a one minute report on a Rovers home game for the Saturday evening programme *Sport in the West*, they introduced me not as John Tidmarsh but as John Baldwin. (The *WDP* office was in Baldwin Street.) I was rumbled immediately and, though no direct accusations were made, I knew that my days in Baldwin Street must be numbered.

I was rescued by Frank Gillard, the famous war correspondent, who was then Head of BBC West Region, and Stuart Wyton, the news editor. They told me that, working as a freelance, I could have my own desk in the tiny newsroom and also become the presenter of the weekly magazine programme *The Week in the West*. They promised to make sure I would not starve and, to bolster my income, they gave me the job of rising early several mornings a week to collect and read the regional weather forecast plus a trailer for forthcoming programmes that same day.

I look back on the four years or so I worked out of the BBC in Whiteladies Road, Bristol, as some of the most enjoyable in a career that would last uninterrupted for nearly fifty years. To begin with it was the company. Anyone who knew Stuart Wyton the news editor, would remember him with great affection; he was good humoured and fun to work with. Alas, he died of cancer much too young.

I last saw him during some rather noisy times in Belfast at the beginning of 'The Troubles' when he was acting as Controller Northern Ireland. His deputy in West Region was an equally relaxed and amiable character, Laurie Mason, who also acted as sports editor.

Then there was what you might call the basic three man field force: Peter Maggs, ex-RAF – I seem to recall he was in Bomber Command in the War – and, from Truro in Cornwall, the rich authentic voice of the West Country, that wonderful broadcaster Tom Salmon. Backing up our five man news team were various other freelance contributors, among them Graham Russell, an old school friend and former colleague on the *WDP*, who often helped to prepare the nightly news bulletin.

My place at the *WDP* was taken by an extremely promising youth with, apparently, ambitions to be a playwright. He may have been working already on a play involving two Shakespeare characters, Rosencrantz and Guildenstern. His name was Tom Stoppard.

Those of us constantly out and about were covering a vast and hugely attractive area of Britain. BBC West Region stretched from Portsmouth and Southampton on the English Channel coast right across to Gloucestershire and the River Severn and included everything south of that line: Gloucestershire, Hampshire, Wiltshire, Dorset, Somerset, Devon and Cornwall. Just for good measure it also took in the Channel Islands. The various strategically placed OB (Outside Broadcast) Units were an essential part of the operation. Their huge black Humber limousines were still in service. On the spot recordings were cut on vinyl discs from equipment in the back seat and then, if urgent, played up the line from the nearest terminal to a studio at headquarters. Similar techniques, with similar vehicles, had been used during the war by some of the BBC's most famous war correspondents, all of whom I worked with at some stage: Richard Dimbleby, Bob Reid, Godfrey Talbot and Frank Gillard, who had been personally told by Field Marshal Montgomery to stay close to him. Monty knew the value of being heard regularly.

Although most of our coverage was to reflect life in the West Region there were moments when star personalities paid us a visit. I may have missed out with Noel Coward but I did get an interview with the Russian composer Khachaturian when he came to Bristol for a concert at the Colston Hall. Southampton was also a rich source of the comings and goings of star personalities from films and politics and sport. In those days it was not the airlines that carried the bulk of the traffic back and forth across the Atlantic but the great ocean liners.

When we were concentrating on regional affairs we seldom missed an opportunity to cover an event celebrating the life of the author Thomas Hardy. We were never short of the best possible advice on the background to his stories set in Dorset for Desmond Hawkins, who followed Frank Gillard as Controller West Region, was internationally famous as a leading authority on Hardy. He also dramatised some of Hardy's novels for radio.

Certain important annual events also found a regular place in our Friday night programme: the summer solstice at Stonehenge, the annual parade of the Padstowe Hobby Horse in Cornwall when, as tradition had it, a man pranced about inside the costume trying to pull young maidens in to join him. Such was our enthusiasm for events steeped in West Country folklore that Peter Maggs once made up a short list of completely bogus ceremonies. My favourite was 'The annual day for crundling the oak apples under Molecatchers' Oak'.

There were times when one or two items featured in *The Week in the West* could be extremely parochial. For example, the story of the Boy Scouts at a place called Langton Matravers completing the building of their own Scout Hut. The piece ended with a line that Tom Salmon and I never forgot. 'Well done, Langton Matravers,' I heard myself saying. Did I actually write that?

The richness of these West Country names made me think at one time how splendid they would be for the characters in a Victorian melodrama. Blandford Forum would be the handsome young hero, Cerne Abbas the villain. And Langton Matravers? A leading member of the judiciary – Mr Justice Langton Matravers.

Famous names, famous faces. A good many were often seen coming and going at the BBC in Whiteladies Road. Field Marshal Montgomery did a series on military campaigns. Long before he was famous, Benny Hill was linked to an outline treatment for a comedy programme, although it was never taken up.

The head of light entertainment in Bristol, Duncan Wood, was always good company. He moved later to London to become the producer of *Hancock's Half Hour*. The absolutely irrepressible Johnny Morris was an almost constant presence, as was the naturalist Peter Scott. I remember seeing Scott one evening sitting at the far end of the club bar and seeming to be in much need of an underarm deodorant. Then we discovered he had a tiny orphaned fox cub cuddled up inside his jacket. Scott was at the time developing his now world famous bird sanctuary at Slimbridge in South Gloucestershire.

I can remember a great deal of laughter during those years in Bristol, not least when a woman taking part in the weekly gardening programme told the other members of the team, 'I spent the week picking the greenfly out of her brassicas.' How the others carried on without exploding I will never know. You could hear that some of them came very close. We dined out on that celebrated broadcasting moment for some time.

There was also the announcer, Douglas Leach, who came on the air at five to six to say: 'This is the West of England Home Service. Now here is the regional weather forecast.' Then, breaking into an extremely broad West Country accent he added: 'Tisn't very good, m'dears.'

Part of my social life after work still took place in The Artichoke on Christmas Steps. It was there I met Pat Pleasance, a fairly new and extremely attractive newcomer to the Rapier Players at the Little Theatre. Romance blossomed and we got married in 1955.

Pat and I were divorced more than thirty years ago, but we are often together. We tell our friends we only got divorced for tax purposes!

During the early fifties I had joined the BBC staff as the representative organising coverage across the region for BBC Television News. But it was working for radio that first put me in direct contact with the principal nightly news programme, the seven o'clock round up of interviews and correspondents' reports from around the world. It went out on the Light Programme and was called *Radio Newsreel.*

It was when there had been severe flooding in Hampshire that I set off one morning with an OB Engineer in one of those historic black Humber recording cars. Soon after six that evening we had cut four discs in the back of the car containing interviews and eye witness accounts of what had happened during a terrible storm the previous night.

The next problem was how to get the material to Broadcasting House in London. Our best hope was a nearby military base where they would probably be able to help us set up a direct line. We were still sending the fourth disc when the first one started coming back on the air right at the beginning of *Radio Newsreel.* The other three duly followed.

That was typical of *Radio Newsreel.* Never the quiet life. No matter what had already been prepared for seven o'clock, if something livelier came in they would throw everything out and make up the rest of the programme as they went along. It could be quite hair raising sometimes, especially when you remember that editing a disc on air in the studio involved marking the grooves with a yellow pencil and relying on the studio manager to lift up the needle manually to leap from one groove to the next. Tremendous team work was required.

2

Next Stop London – Then NY!

It was in the summer of 1956 that I found myself working for *Radio Newsreel* on a regular basis. No longer in Bristol I had accepted the invitation to become a staff reporter with BBC News Division at Broadcasting House at the top of Regent Street. To say the least resources were a bit overstretched in covering both the Anglo-French action in Suez and the Soviet invasion of Hungary to prevent its breaking away from the Communist bloc.

I remember some of those pictures of Hungarian citizens, sometimes whole families, fleeing to freedom across the border with Austria. Some of those people I would be meeting later when they arrived in America. The person reporting those dramatic scenes on the Austro-Hungarian border was one of the BBC's greatest correspondents, Charles Wheeler. Just before Charles died in 2008 at the age of 85 I had been trying to set up a nostalgic reunion over lunch with two former women members of the Paris office we had both known during spells of duty in France helping out another great BBC correspondent, Thomas Cadett.

It was in that autumn of 1956 that I spent a great deal of time going back and forth to London Airport to interview various VIPs, coming and going, about these two great crises. After one of these excursions I returned to BH to find a slightly agitated Reporting Organiser, Waldo Maguire, demanding to know where I had been.

'The Airport,' I said, 'where you sent me.'

He told me to go home and get my passport so that they could arrange a visa for the United States. I then had to see Sister for a smallpox vaccination.

'We are sending you tonight to New York to work at United Nations.'

What!

Apparently the UN correspondent, F.D. Walker (Dick Walker), and the two Washington correspondents, Christopher Serpell and Douglas Willis, were all close to exhaustion, having to cover long, sometimes all-night, sessions of the Security Council. It was also the annual meeting of the General Assembly. Normally, a back up special correspondent would have been there already, staying for three or four months until the Assembly was over. Hardiman Scott (Peter Scott) had been earmarked for the job, but he had been sent to back up the Suez operation and was based for the moment in Cyprus. It was tough luck on Peter, an extremely experienced journalist and broadcaster and a great colleague. As for me, after only two or three months in London, I was about to get my first experience as a foreign correspondent.

That night a car collected me to rush me out to the airport (my second visit of the day). I had been given a first class ticket with a sleeping berth on board one of those lovely old, four engined Stratocruisers, flown on the Atlantic route by BOAC.

The Jet Age had not yet arrived and, because it was not possible to fly directly between London and New York, our first stop would be Gandar in Newfoundland. It turned out to be more of an unscheduled stop-over than a stop. I was fast asleep in my very spacious bed – it pulled down from what in today's aircraft is the overhead luggage rack – when one of the cabin staff gently shook me awake to tell me that I would have to get up. Apparently, some 400 miles from Gandar, out over the Atlantic, an engine had failed. It would have to be replaced, which meant we were now likely to be in Gandar for at least twenty-four hours. We first class passengers were put up in a very comfortable hotel and, shortly after breakfast the following morning, seat belts fastened, we were picking up speed for take-off when the captain suddenly applied the brakes. A further adjustment was needed on the new engine. We eventually reached New York more than a day late.

If you are coming to that great city for the first time you must try to arrive, as I did, as daylight is beginning to fade. The sun is below the western horizon and the lights of the skyscrapers in mid-town Manhattan have come on against the pale blue, slowly darkening backcloth of twilight. It is a magnificent spectacle.

Twilight is a magic time in New York – and elsewhere in America. Was it not the Sage of Baltimore, H.L. Mencken, who said: 'The most magic sound in America is the tinkle of ice tumbling into a glass at twilight'? I had already made a vow to celebrate my arrival in New York with my first authentic Dry Martini (a very generous measure of gin and go easy with the martini).

As one of the first to appoint a permanent correspondent at the United Nations the BBC had secured a very attractive office. C310 was close to the Security Council and General Assembly alongside the tower block. One window, the width of the whole room, looked out onto the East River. Sitting at one of the desks trying to work, I was constantly distracted as the bow of a ship would appear at the starboard edge of the window and pass slowly by until the stern disappeared from view on the port side.

Dick Walker was very amiable and good humoured, but often gave the impression that he was not very keen on broadcasting. Whenever possible he gave me the job of voicing a despatch to London for the main news and programmes like *Radio Newsreel.*

He was at home catching up with some of the sleep he had lost before my arrival, when I picked up a huge story. The Secretary-General, Dag Hammarskjold, had been asked by the Security Council for his thoughts on extricating Britain and France from what was now seen as the acutely embarrassing Suez operation. Hammarskjold, a Swedish diplomat, was already lending the job of Secretary-General more stature and more importance while at the same time enhancing the rôle of the United Nations. The report that landed in our office that morning presented a detailed review of the situation for several pages.

On the final page was the big story. He was suggesting the formation of a UN force to replace the British and French – the very first Blue Berets.

When the Security Council and the General Assembly had cooled down a little I was asked to go down to a military camp in New Jersey to pursue a story linked to the Hungarian Revolution. That was where I met some of those refugees Charles Wheeler had seen escaping from Budapest and other parts of the country. They were now cheerfully looking forward to a new life in America. I was with a UN official who was taking them a large number of English-Hungarian dictionaries.

Once I knew that I would be in America for several months – probably until February the following year – Pat came out to join me. I had found us a very attractive, small apartment – bedroom, bathroom, living room, small kitchen concealed in a cupboard – on East 40th between Park and Lexington; it was rather a posh address. From there we led a very full social life. Pat must have seen nearly a dozen Broadway productions. When work allowed, I joined her. We saw *Damn Yankees*, *Most Happy Fella*, *Lil Abner* and a great production of *Inherit the Wind*, a show based on what was known as 'The Monkey Trial', in which a Southern teacher is accused of promoting Darwin's theory of evolution. Paul Muni starred as the great defence lawyer Clarence Darrow, with Ed Begley as his opponent for the prosecution.

In those days the BBC's Head Office in America was very grand. On one of the higher floors of the Rockefeller Building on Fifth Avenue it looked down on the spires of St Patrick's Cathedral. The man who greatly enjoyed representing the BBC right across America was Barrie Thorne. We found him wonderful company, not least because he also came from Bristol. He was certainly an enthusiastic entertainer on the BBC's behalf, never short of an excuse to throw a party in his sumptuous apartment on the East Side, close to Central Park.

On one very memorable evening the guests of honour were from the Broadway production of *My Fair Lady*, one of the shows we could never get in to see during the entire four months we were in New York. The lovely Julie Andrews was there. I did a long interview with her many years later when I was with *Outlook*. Then there was someone I noticed almost pinned into a corner of one of the rooms by a crowd of admirers. It was Stanley Holloway who played the dustman, Alfred Doolittle, Julie's father.

Because of the time difference between London and New York most of our evenings were free – certainly when the tumult over Suez eventually died down. In any case, getting a link to London for a piece in broadcast quality was not straightforward, involving, as it did, booking a circuit on the Trans-Atlantic cable. Moreover, there were not the multitude of round the clock demands that must often make the life of today's correspondents such a misery. Assuming London was quietly tucked up in bed, we usually went out to enjoy ourselves.

From time to time we spent an evening on the town with Joanna Van Damm and her husband. She was our secretary at the UN and virtually ran the place. At the end of each week she would present me with a sheet of paper saying: 'Sign this, John, your expenses.' She had done them all for me.

We made one other lasting friendship in America. His name was Bill Parish, a prize winning producer with CBS. We met at one of Barrie Thorne's parties. Bill was in the US Airforce during the war and claimed to be the only pilot who crash landed twice on the same day. On the second effort he destroyed half his station's chicken farm which made him rather less than a popular hero! I seem to remember he flew Thunderbolts. Some years later he helped to fly a squadron of elderly World War II bombers across the Atlantic for a film being made in Europe by Cubby Broccoli.

During the Nixon administration he became for a while the Photographic Editor in the White House, but then left to do the same job for the department that deals with America's great outdoors. So he missed the Watergate scandal which led to Nixon's downfall.

His final job took him back once more to the White House, again as Photographic Editor, this time for Jimmy Carter. He was actually in the White House when he had a massive heart attack and died. It was President Carter himself who asked the family if they would like to bury him in Washington's historic Arlington Cemetery – which is where he lies today.

After four hugely enjoyable months in New York it was something of a wrench when the time came to go back to London. I had almost begun to think of myself as a New Yorker. From the moment I arrived everything about the place and the American way of life seemed so familiar, and not just from all the movies I had seen in the forties and fifties, when we went to the 'pictures' usually once a week.

This was America where the music still came from the Big Swing Bands: the Dorsey Brothers, Tommy and Jimmy, Artie Shaw, Benny

Goodman, the Glenn Miller Orchestra; the songs from great songwriters like George Gershwin, Irving Berlin, Cole Porter and Jerome Kern. (Strange to think that poor Glenn Miller never left our shores. It is now thought his plane went down on a flight to France in 1944 when it entered an area not far from Newhaven on the English Channel coast. This was where bombers returning from rearranging Germany dropped anything they had left in the bomb bay.)

In the final stages of the Second World War I became greatly addicted to AFN, the American Forces Network based in Munich. It was there I heard, not just the music I love, but also some of those great radio comedies: Burns and Allen, the incomparable Jack Benny and the weekly visit to Duffy's Tavern, which always began with a voice answering the telephone: 'Duffy's Tavern. Archie, the manager, speaking. Duffy ain't here yet.' As far as I remember, Duffy was never there.

Then there was television, with a huge number of available stations sustained by all too frequent breaks for advertising. A toothpaste ad. was one I have never forgotten: 'You'll wonder where the yellow went when you go steady with Pepsodent.' It was something we were just beginning to see in Britain with the start of ITV. But if many of the programmes were unwatchable – and I had better things to do – there were at least times when one or other of the stations would be running an old film.

I lost count over the four months of the number of times we could have seen one of my all time favourites: *Mr Blandings Builds His Dreamhouse*, starring Myrna Loy and that well-known Bristolian, Cary Grant. (I met Cary when he was visiting his mother, who lived just round the corner from our house in Henleaze. Did she still call him Archie? His real name was Archie Leach.)

Looking back all these years later we can now see how the great music and the songs of the first half of the 20th century were about to be almost drowned out by Rock and Roll, which also put an end to ballroom dancing as we knew it. No more gliding silkily across the floor to the waltz or the quick-step, holding your partner around the waist. In madder, jazzier moments we had also learnt to jive and jitterbug. The American servicemen brought that style of dance to Britain in the Second World War. Now, however, it was 'tribal' dancing

– much uncontrolled waving of the arms along with twisting and girating the body. You had a partner but you hardly touched each other.

The mid-fifties also marked the decline of another great institution: Tin Pan Alley. The original was on 28th St, between Sixth Avenue and Broadway, in New York. But it subsequently became the unofficial nickname for streets in cities all over America where the publishers of sheet music set up their offices.

So, farewell, New York. But only for a brief absence. I have been back many times. In later years, my voice was heard three days a week right across America, from WBUR in Boston to KALW in San Francisco, when American Public Radio decided they liked *Outlook* and re-broadcast it every week-day from BBC World Service.

My long attachment to World Service, lasting for more than thirty years, was still some way off when I finally got back to London. Then, after having enjoyed one of the very best overseas postings in the gift of BBC News Division, I suddenly found myself working once again as a local, regional reporter.

In the mid-fifties reporters working for BBC News Division were all based at Egton House, next door to Broadcasting House, just behind All Souls' Church. Television News was still in what I call the years BC (Before Colour). When it started up again, just after the war, at Alexandra Palace in North London, faces were not seen.

The first part was a bulletin read by a newsreader from Radio concealed behind maps, diagrams and still pictures, apparently for fear that, if we saw his face we might be able to tell what he was thinking. The second half of the nightly news was film with a commentary rather like the old cinema newsreels. But now Television News decided they wanted a corps of their own reporters. Goodness knows why! They certainly had very little idea of what to do with us.

I say 'us' because, along with Hardiman Scott and Donald Milner, I was chosen to go to 'Ally Pally' as we called it. None of us was very enthused and no-one more horrified than the film editors. The idea that they might be forced to put 'talking heads' on a screen that should be devoted almost entirely to moving pictures was to them totally abhorrent. We did sometimes appear very briefly doing what were called 'noddies' or 'cutaways', when no other way could be found to edit an interview. In those days it was all black and white film, usually 16mm., which was first developed, then edited by cutting it and sticking the bits together again – very cumbersome.

However, I would appear regularly on the screen two or three days a week, but only in London and South East England, in the weeknight programme that followed the main news, then being read in vision by Bob Dougall, Richard Baker or Kenneth Kendall. It was called *Town and Around.*

When it came to the 'Around' bit I found myself doing nearly all the leg work, but I had some splendid company as fellow presenters. Firstly, there was the lovely Nan Winton, who would later become, albeit briefly, the first woman to read the main national news. The 'boss class' quickly decided it was not a job for a woman! Only men could project the necessary 'authority'. Today there often seem to be more women reading the news than men. Another presenter, also fun to be with, was John Ellison, a very well-known voice as presenter of the extremely popular Saturday night radio programme, *In Town Tonight.* Outside Broadcasts were in charge of production and one of the regular contributors, 'live' from somewhere in London, was one of my favourite broadcasters, Brian Johnston, universally known as 'Johnners'. He went on to become one of the best loved cricket commentators. Whenever I had occasion to call him up 'live' to check on the latest score for a programme I was presenting he always called me 'Tidders', the nickname that stuck with me for virtually all my career.

I suppose many people these days would think that appearing regularly on television, even just in one of the Regions, was a wonderful opportunity. I didn't. Radio seemed to offer many more opportunities for someone like me with ambitions to work abroad. I asked to be sent back to Egton House. It was a good moment to choose.

There was a lot going on in 1958. France, for example, came within a whisker of civil war over the future of Algeria. At the time I don't think many people knew just how close Paris came to being invaded by paratroopers from Algeria and Toulouse before President René Coty asked General de Gaulle to form a new government and the National Assembly voted in favour. At that moment I was not in Algeria but at the other end of the Mediterranean. I had left London *en route* for Cyprus, which had become a thoroughly dangerous place. Acts of sabotage and attacks against British troops as EOKA, led by a Greek Cypriot called George Grivas, tried to liberate the island from British rule and establish union with Greece. I got as far as Athens, checked into one of the best hotels in the city, and woke up the following morning to find a cable had been slipped under my door while I was asleep.

It simply said: 'Proceed Beirut soonest.' Lebanon was also on the verge of all-out civil war. Attempts were being made to overthrow the Maronite Christian President, Camille Chamoun, by pan-Arabists, encouraged by President Nasser of Egypt. I quickly discovered that Beirut could be quite noisy at night with the persistent rattle of automatic weapons, but quite normal in daylight hours as the citizens went about their daily business. It was rather civilised really, with nothing much going on until after dinner. Along with a few other correspondents, including Reggie Bosanquet from ITN, I stayed in the luxurious St George Hotel on the sea front. It overlooked a splendid beach thronged with bathers and sun-bathers.

It was on an afternoon in June that I beheld the most bizarre spectacle. Chamoun had asked America for help. Suddenly the US Navy appeared just off shore to land the Marines. Bathers and sunbathers looked on in some astonishment. Then followed a delicious moment when one of the Marines bearing a very heavy back-pack stumbled and fell to his knees in the water just a few yards from the shore. Immediately, two of the bathers went to his assistance and helped him to his feet. It was a picture that must have appeared in newspapers all over the world. Ultimately Chamoun resigned and General Chehab took over, a leader more acceptable to the Muslim community.

The big story in the Middle East was now Iraq. On the 14th of July young King Faisal was murdered, along with most of his family, and General Abdul Karim Qaism became the first Prime Minister of the Republic of Iraq. I was told to get to Baghdad 'soonest'.

Leaving Beirut one morning just after breakfast I got as far as Damascus, where I had to change planes. After studying my passport the Syrian authorities decided to deport me on the excuse that I didn't have a transit visa. So I was back again in Beirut in time for lunch. Shortly after that Erik de Mauny, who knew much more about the Middle East than I did, made a second attempt and managed to get through. I, however, was soon on my way back to London.

I took with me another delicious moment to remember from those days in Beirut. One morning at a news conference in the US Embassy one of the visiting correspondents asked for some more detailed political guidance on the current situation and the likely outcome. The Embassy spokesman advised him to read what he called an 'extremely perceptive report' written by one of the other correspondents in the room, who was representing the London newspaper, *The Sunday Observer*. The correspondent's name was Kim Philby. It was from Beirut that Philby, 'The Third Man', eventually disappeared, to turn up later in Moscow, joining in exile the two other Cambridge Soviet agents who had earlier fled from London, Burgess and MacLean.

In the years between 1958 and 1962 I greatly enjoyed a number of opportunities to be sent to France to help out in the Paris office. This was the base for, as I mentioned earlier, one of the greatest and best informed BBC correspondents, Thomas Cadett. Tom had been working in Paris before the war and, when it was all over, he was able to re-establish himself in the wonderful apartment he had had, overlooking the Bois de Bolougne. A photograph of the high ranking German officer who had lived in Tom's flat during the occupation of France now hung on the back of the lavatory door.

In his book on de Gaulle, *The Last Great Frenchman*, Charles Williams quotes a comment made in the 18th century by that great Parliamentarian, Edmund Burke: 'It is the nature of all greatness not to be exact.' How well de Gaulle needed to echo that thought when, shortly after taking power, he made his visit to Algeria in June 1958. The French settlers in Algeria, the Pieds-Noirs, were hoping that he, like them, wanted Algeria to remain part of France. Nevertheless, when he spoke to a huge crowd in Algiers, it is believed that a sniper was waiting to assassinate him if he said the wrong thing. To a wildly cheering crowd he simply said, 'I have understood you.'

We now know that what he himself already 'understood' was the impossibility of keeping Algeria as a part of Metropolitan France while the two countries on either side in North Africa, Tunisia and

Morocco, were independent. Briefly, though, the Pieds-Noirs, were able to believe he was on their side.

The Army in Algeria also thought they had avoided the one solution they dreaded: surrender to the people they had been fighting the, FLN, the Algerian rebels. The army's humiliation in Vietnam at Dien Bien Phu was still too dreadful a memory to make that an acceptable outcome. Yet, three years later, it was the French armed forces in Algeria that brought France once again to the verge of civil war.

In January 1961 de Gaulle organised a referendum on self-determination for Algeria. It won the support of more than 75 per cent of the voters. The supporters of a French Algeria were bitterly angry and in April a number of officers, among them General Salan and General Jouhaud, seized power in Algiers. De Gaulle went on television, wearing his uniform as Commander of the Armed Forces, to denounce this attempted *coup d'état* and to appeal for the support of the French people. 'Francaises, Francais! Aidez moi.'

It was at this moment that I was despatched from London to drive down to Marseilles to await the invasion. Before leaving I was greatly touched by the Foreign Editor, the amiable Tony Wigan, saying to me, 'John, you will be careful won't you. We'd be very upset if you got killed.'

I remember replying, 'Don't worry, Tony. I'd be very annoyed myself.'

Should the invasion take place and normal communications break down, I was told I would have to drive along the Cote d'Azur into Italy to send my despatches. In reality I spent a most enjoyable week in Marseilles. I somehow found something to report to *Radio Newsreel* every evening: the tension in Marseilles; the ferocious intervention of the CRS, the Riot Police, whenever a demonstration against de Gaulle seemed imminent. Most evenings I dined in the open air at one of those lovely restaurants which used to encircle the Vieux Port. It was there that I first enjoyed *bouillabaisse* and also what became one of my favourite fish dishes: grilled *loup de mer*, or sea bass. The biggest alarm came one night, around four o'clock in the morning, when everyone in my hotel, which included other journalists, was woken by an enormous explosion. We all leapt out of bed, thinking the invasion had begun. But it was just the start of a very noisy thunderstorm.

Subsequently, when the immediate crisis was deemed to be over, I was called back to Paris, soon to be the scene of acts of terrorism and sabotage and attempts to assassinate de Gaulle as the supporters of a French Algeria formed the Organisation de l'Armée Secrète (OAS).

My next link with the Algeria story came a year later when I was sent to Evian on Lake Geneva to report the formal talks that would lead to Algerian independence. Many check points in and around Evian ensured maximum security while the talks were in process, although the Algerian delegation lived on the other side of the Lake in Switzerland, crossing each day by boat. This involved a slight hold-up one day when the Lake was a bit rough; the Algerian leader, Belkacem Krim, arrived somewhat the worse for wear, having been very sea sick. As a result, the talks were adjourned for twenty-four hours. Eventually, on the 18th of March 1962, the Evian Accords were signed bringing an end to hostilities and giving independence to Algeria.

My own association with this story would finally end in 1962 with my first ever visit to Algeria itself. The tension was almost visible on Independence Day. Suddenly came news that many people had been killed as crowds thronged the main streets in Oran, the second city. Shots had been fired, possibly in jubilation. Unfortunately, it had caused a wholesale panic. Next morning I set off to reach Oran by road in the company of a French photographer who drove one of those little 2CVs. The closer we got to Oran the fewer people seemed to be around. Then we started running into check points, manned by the former FLN who were now in charge of security. At each stop I detected, partly hidden from view, a man with an automatic weapon focused on us and our car. But a press pass was always enough to see us through. Eventually we arrived in Oran where, once again, the tension – the fear even – was almost visible.

Checking into a hotel in a quiet square, just off one of the city's main roads, I met a couple who were to become good friends. Paul Davies was an American television camera man; his Belgian wife, Monique, working alongside him. He had already solved what was always a major problem in those days: communication. With the permission of the hotel manager he had taken over the telephone box on the first floor of the hotel and turned it into a very basic studio. I could now speak fairly clearly to Foreign News and *Radio*

Newsreel in London, and one or two other journalists, among them the *Daily Express* correspondent, could record their despatches in Broadcasting House to be collected later by their own newsrooms.

Oran became even more creepy at night with dark and almost deserted streets. Paul and Monique had with them their own pet dachshund known as Adia, so the three of us took Adia for her evening 'walkies', talking rather loudly in English as we went, until we found one of the restaurants that was open until the nightly curfew.

Just a few miles outside Oran the scene was very different. France had retained the right to continue using the naval base at Mers El Kebir. Once you passed through the main gates it was another world – just like being back in France itself. The lights were on, cafés were open, crowded with people eating and drinking in the open air on a lovely warm evening.

I was based in Oran just long enough to witness a very joyful scene for the Algerians. One day I took the short journey to Tlemcen on the Moroccan frontier. There hundreds of people were lining the street to see the man who was the acknowledged leader of the struggle for Algeria's independence as he finally returned to become the country's first president. His name was Ahmed Ben Bella. The mere sight of him sent the crowd into raptures. Although he had spent the last six years in prison in France he was still recognised and revered as a founder member in 1954 of the National Liberation Front (the FLN).

After being arrested by the French in 1952 he escaped and fled to Cairo and worked to supply the FLN with arms. He was actually in Morocco when the French re-captured him after he boarded a plane in Rabat. Four French agents also got on board and managed to divert the aircraft to Algiers where Ben Bella and three associates travelling with him were all arrested.

In spite of the delirium on that day in Tlemcen, Ben Bella was president for only two years. In 1965 he was overthrown in a coup led by the Army Chief, Colonel Boumedienne. For fifteen years he was held under house arrest before he was allowed to leave to live in exile in Switzerland, returning only briefly at the beginning of the nineties to make an unsuccessful bid for power.

1962 turned out to be the year of one of my greatest adventures working for BBC Foreign News. It was the year when we all wondered whether we would ever see another. In October the Cuban Missile Crisis brought us to the brink of nuclear war. That final week-end in October time seemed to be running out. Looking up from our office window in BH on Friday afternoon into the blue skies above London, I wondered whether one would ever see a nuclear missile coming in. Remembering the V2s at the end of the Second World War I thought it unlikely. There would be that split second as the device exploded – then oblivion.

That week-end I went home with two airline tickets in my pocket. One was for Washington if war started, though what I was supposed to do, even if I managed to get there, I have never really quite fathomed. Thankfully, Khrushchev came to his senses and ordered the Soviet ships carrying missiles to Cuba to turn round and return home. So I sent the Washington air ticket back to the office and on Sunday checked in on the other flight, non-stop to Delhi. Pakistan and India were at war over Kashmir and our Delhi correspondent, Ivor Jones, needed some back-up.

Next morning I woke up as the flight moved in across the sub-continent and found myself looking down on the glorious Himalayas and the region where my father served in the Indian Army all those years ago. Very quickly the focus of attention moved away from the fighting in Kashmir to the other end of the Himalayas and India's frontier with China. In support of their Pakistani friends the Chinese were moving troops up to the Indian border with the clear threat of invading.

All Indian internal passenger flights across to the other side of the sub-continent were cancelled in order for troop reinforcements to be sent to the region. Initially there was some talk of my taking Ivor's car and driver for the journey. The driver, the delightful Ram, got rather excited, suggesting to me that we take some guns to do some hunting on the way. I gently explained that this was probably not quite what Foreign News in London had in mind.

In any case, Ivor was obviously keen to retain both his car and driver and also to remain in Delhi, where he had one or two permanently booked circuits to London each week so that his authoritative voice might still be heard regularly on *Radio Newsreel* and other news programmes. Ivor certainly liked to be sure the listeners could never forget him and his importance to BBC News output. I had no option but to try to get across India and up into the Himalayas on my own, initially to a place called Tezpur on the Brahmaputra River, where correspondents were already gathering in the hope of being taken up closer to the frontier. What a wonderful opportunity!

In the first place I had to find some way of getting to the great city of Calcutta. There was only one way to do it: an international flight. So I bought a ticket with Air France from Delhi to Bangkok, enjoying an excellent breakfast in First Class – no seats were available in Economy! After an excellent lunch in Bangkok I hopped onto another First Class flight, this time with Pan Am, to take me to Calcutta in time for dinner in a lovely hotel on the Chowringee. When it was urgent to get there one did not bother too much about the cost – at least, not in those days.

Next morning, very early, I stepped out of the hotel into a smog. All along the covered sidewalk were bundles of heavily wrapped human beings – just a few of the city's homeless. The fog had come from their small, individual fires, lit to keep them warm and cook whatever bits and pieces of food they had been able to scrounge.

Short flights in small aircraft were still operating and at Dum Dum airport I was able to find one going to Gauhati, close to the Brahmaputra. From there I went in search of a car hire firm that would drive me along the south bank of the river to Tezpur. I had been recommended a company run by an actor who was currently 'resting' as they say in the profession. When I told him where I was going and why he said he would be my driver as it sounded rather interesting. We agreed to set off around dawn the following morning and I booked for the night into what has always remained for me one of the most delightful places I have ever stayed.

They put me in one of the self-contained bungalows in the hotel grounds. Living room, bedroom and bathroom. The living room had an open fire and late in the afternoon a knock on the door announced a small boy carrying a basket of coal wanting to know 'if Sahib would like a fire'. Sahib would indeed. Nights can be a bit chilly in those parts. The region could well have been one of those places where, in the days of the Raj, the memsahibs were sent to avoid the intense summer heat down on the plains.

That evening, after dinner, I sat in a comfortable chair beside the fire, book in one hand, generous glass of whisky in the other, wondering why on earth Capt. Charles Tidmarsh had ever left the Indian Army. Too late now to ask him. He had died a few months earlier in the summer of 1962. I had never been able to persuade him to tell me very much about his days in India.

As arranged, my car came for me at dawn and we set off to drive along the south bank of the Brahmaputra. As we came closer to Tezpur I told the driver that, once we crossed to the other bank of the River – the Tezpur side – it might be difficult to find somewhere to stay.

'I can sort that out,' he said. 'The manager of the ferry is a friend of mine.'

The ferry consisted of two large, sternwheel paddle steamers, one of them moored to the bank on the Tezpur side as the manager's headquarters. I was immediately made welcome and told that I could have the cabin at the stern of the boat, which comprised a spacious bedroom, bathroom and loo. I stayed aboard for two or three days, waking each morning to a knock on the door as a Nepalese steward asked if Sahib would like his morning tea and then his breakfast in his cabin or out on the after deck. Not a difficult choice on a glorious, warm and sunny morning. Eventually, I found somewhere decent to stay on shore in Tezpur, joining in the general clamour among all the other journalists to get the Indian Army to take us up to some nine or ten thousand feet and the threatened frontier.

This part of the North East Frontier was normally closed to visitors to allow the tribes people who lived at this altitude, the Monpas, traditionally Tibetan Buddhists by religion, to go on leading their simple lives as farmers, breeding yaks and sheep. At lower, warmer altitudes, closer to Tezpur and the Brahmaputra, they also planted crops.

Finally, the Indian Army received the go-ahead from Delhi to take a party up the narrow and precarious road to the pass at Bomdi La and on northwards to the Buddhist monastery at Tawang. It was right on the border and had in the past been part of Tibet and Bhutan.

It was at this moment that Ludovic Kennedy turned up. He was working for the current affairs television programme *Panorama*. The BBC was greatly respected in India, so Ludo and I were put into the jeep at the head of the convoy, with a driver and the Indian major who had been given the job of leading the expedition.

It was without a doubt one of the most spectacular journeys I have ever taken. Not only was the road just about wide enough for one vehicle, though with passing places at regular intervals, but, sitting on the right hand side of the rear passenger seats, I found I was often looking into an abyss. One false move and you could be plunging hundreds of feet to your death, almost vertically down the densely forested mountainside. Every so often we came to a spot where some tragedy must have taken place, marked by a small pile of stones erected as a monument to the dead. The drop was so fearsome it was probably impossible to recover any bodies.

Once or twice we saw one of the Monpas, dressed in maroon robes, and giving us that traditional, peaceful greeting with the hands held in front of the face, palms together as if in prayer, to say 'Welcome and have a safe journey'. We saw very few signs along the route of villages or settlements. When we did it was the tall poles that caught the eye, each bearing many prayer flags fluttering horizontally in the mountain breeze to send their messages up to the heavens. The people themselves seemed anxious to keep a low profile, no doubt worried about what might happen to disturb the peace and their way of life.

Just before we reached Bomdi La we ran into a problem that greatly annoyed our major. At one of the passing places some down traffic had come a little too far and was blocking our way. Leaping out of the jeep the major ran off to try and sort it out. It didn't take him long and as we prepared to move again, onward and upward, he returned to the vehicle and remarked, in the perfect tones of an officer trained at Sandhurst, 'Dear God! I've never seen such a bugger's muddle in all my life.'

We greatly enjoyed the major's company, not least when an American correspondent asked him about the small tiger heads denoting his rank on his shoulder flashes. 'Well,' he explained, 'when we became independent we had to get rid of the crowns we wore in the British Indian Army. We decided to replace them with these pussycats.'

We spent the night at the base in Bomdi La, enjoying a very sociable evening in the temporary officers' mess, then sleeping on straw filled mattresses in sleeping bags to keep us warm. Early next morning we were off again, stopping to pay our respects to the Abbot of Tawang, as we neared the frontier. It was already clear that the Indian troops would be no match for the Chinese if they invaded. They seemed very ill-equipped, having only ancient Lee Enfield rifles. Many having been rushed up from the plains, were also suffering from altitude sickness.

One particular scene has always stuck in my mind. It was misty, with cloud swirling round the mountain top, when a shaft of sunlight lit up the area where I was standing. Out of the mist came a mule; then another and another – maybe half a dozen altogether – driven on by a single soldier. Strapped to the side of each mule were boxes containing ammunition and, no doubt, more ancient rifles. It could have been a scene from the Spanish Civil War nearly thirty years earlier.

Suddenly the major was rounding us all up and we began the journey back down to Tezpur. Going down seemed much quicker than going up and we were back again in Tezpur on the Brahmaputra without an overnight stop. This was just as well as the Chinese had finally invaded, some of their troops circling through Bhutan to cut the road at Bomdi La only a few hours after we had gone through. But for a fortuitous piece of timing, Ludo and I might have found ourselves prisoners of the Chinese People's Liberation Army. I am not sure the initials 'BBC' would have counted for much.

However, my job now was to get back down to Calcutta and do some broadcasting. I did manage to get through to London but the quality of the circuit was poor, so my great adventure went out on the air as: 'John Tidmarsh's report from Calcutta is read here in the studio.' Curses! In the meantime the Chinese had gone as far as they wanted, though that was far enough – right down to Tezpur. They then went back home without even bothering to take any of the Indian equipment they had captured, the final insult. It was a huge wake-up call for the Indian Government and the world's arms' salesmen gleefully rubbed their hands at the prospect.

I remained based in Calcutta for the next few days hoping that

London might want me to go back into the mountains again. I was captivated, not just by the awesome beauty of the north eastern end of the Himalayas, but also the spiritual and rather mystical atmosphere of the region and its Tibetan Buddhist culture. If Shangri-La had ever existed – and perhaps we have yet to find it – it would surely be here: the hidden lamasery of James Hilton's book *Lost Horizon* – a gentle, peaceful place, where time stood still.

In 1942, twenty years before I was there, the people of the region were able to witness, and sometimes help, one of the most important operations of the Second World War. It was not going well for the Chinese, important allies in the fight against Japan. General Chiang Kai-shek had been pushed back remorselessly and had created an emergency capital on the upper reaches of the Yangtze river at Chungking.

He urgently needed supplies but the Japanese had already blocked all traditional overland routes for getting them to him. It could only be done by air. This involved loading cargo into those valiant DC-2 and DC-3 twin-engined aircraft and getting them to fly several thousand feet above their normal highest operational altitude in order to clear what came the be called The Hump, the barrier at the eastern end of the Himalayas, which in places touches twenty thousand feet. Over a period of three years it grew to be the biggest supply operation of the Second World War. There were many casualties, both aircraft and crews. If you went down in the Himalayas your chances of getting out alive were pretty bleak. Some did, however, often helped and guided by local tribes people. These survivors eventually formed what they called 'The Walkers Club'.

Two of the men who played a part in this operation would later become the founders of one of the best modern airlines. They were an American called Roy Farrell and an Australian, Sydney de Kantzow. When the war ended they set up a cargo business using the same faithful aircraft that had flown The Hump. Farrell's DC-3 was affectionately known to him as 'Betsy'. This initially modest commercial enterprise eventually became Cathay Pacific.

Alas, I was not sent back to the mountains, though I would be there again just three years later. I was needed for the time being in Delhi, where Ivor was anxious to take some time off. Then it was back again to London. Although I had hugely enjoyed my six weeks in India, I was now greatly looking forward to being back again with the family.

It was Christopher Serpell, the great BBC correspondent in Rome and then Washington, who once told me: 'Just because you are good at the job don't think you are certain to be promoted.' How true. Over the next four years I suffered both frustration and irritation.

My time was now equally divided between Television News at Alexandra Palace, Foreign News, working out of Broadcasting House, and some very enjoyable interludes at Westminster. At one point I rose to the dizzy height of being named the BBC's Scottish Lobby correspondent. Either there were no other volunteers or, for the moment, they couldn't think of anyone else. Working generally in the Lobby was a splendid introduction to the often furtive nature of life in the Westminster village, with its background briefings on a 'don't quote me' basis.

Regular briefing sessions came once a week on a Thursday, in a remote part of the Palace of Westminster, when the Leader of the House gave details of the business planned for the following week.

For 'live' reports into the News, radio and television, the BBC now had a remote control studio, in what looked no larger than a broom cupboard, in a building just across the road from Parliament on the banks of the Thames. I was allowed to do reports for television, but the real stars of the BBC's Westminster team were Conrad Voss Bark and Roland Fox. Conrad, I suspect, would much rather have been fishing; indeed, he used to write a regular fishing column for *The Times*.

I suppose you could say that our legislators were the first to create the British working practice, now pursued much more widely, on a Friday – POETS (Piss off early, tomorrow's Saturday). After the start of Parliament at eleven o'clock it was usually all over for the day, there being nothing much more going on or worth reporting. It was a wonderful opportunity for Roland and me to find one of our favourite watering holes and sink a few pints.

When I went back to general duties with the reporters' unit in BH, London Airport was a still a popular venue for trying to get a few words for the nightly bulletin from some important figure flying in or flying out. Very early in 1963 I had several meetings with Edward Heath, Britain's chief negotiator in the first effort to join what was then called the EEC. It was a contact that would shortly pay tremendous dividends.

On January 29th General de Gaulle made it quite clear that Britain would join the EEC over his dead body, though he did not put it quite so bluntly – and, indeed, de Gaulle was dead and buried before Britain tried again. By this time Edward Heath was Prime Minister.

To cover the final moments of that first application in 1963, I was sent to Brussels with the BBC's great diplomatic correspondent, Tom Barman. I was to look after the demands of Television News, an arrangement that more than suited Tom. Like several of the BBC's top correspondents, Tom regarded Television News with some disdain; it was not a place he would want to work. Radio News was the equivalent of a broadsheet newspaper, Television more like a tabloid. The Assistant Head of News, Stuart Hood, once told some of us reporters working in television that our job could be most closely compared with that of a caption writer on the *Daily Mirror*.

However, the night of January 29th 1963 would allow me to be rather more than that. I had travelled over to Brussels the day before on the famous, and quite luxurious, Night Ferry – one of those glamorous old trains that has long disappeared. We were booked into the Metropole Hotel and Heath gave several of us a briefing before the fatal meeting.

For the six o'clock news on the 29th I was on the air explaining what had happened. The word 'Non' from de Gaulle was a veto for Britain, which the other five nations had to accept. Come back some other time. Early that evening I met Heath in the lobby of the Metropole and asked him if he would come with me at seven o'clock to record an interview over what was then called the Eurovision link. Our circuit time had been booked in advance and would last only half an hour. Heath promised he would try, but he had first to go to another meeting. At 7.00 I was waiting patiently in the lobby. At 7.15 he still hadn't come back. At 7.25 I saw him coming through the revolving doors, grabbed him by the arm and led him to the car we had waiting outside. It was then that I said something rather foolish to the driver.

'Get us to RTB/BRT in Place Eugène Flagy as quickly as you can.'

What a daft thing to say to a Belgian driver! We were both mightily relieved when we arrived safely at the Radio and Television station. Someone back at the Metropole had kindly phoned to say we were on our way and the precious Eurovision link had been held open. Heath was absolutely furious with de Gaulle and it certainly came across.

While he remained President of France there was no point in continuing the negotiations. But Heath insisted there was no question of Britain now turning its back on Europe. The meeting he had attended earlier was with the other five EEC members, and they had all made clear their dismay at de Gaulle's attitude and their determination that Britain would one day become a member. Heath said: 'Millions of people in the European Community – the vast majority – want us to join.'

Having secured the only interview for television (and radio) that evening – a 'scoop' you might say – I returned to London to warm congratulations from the 'Top Brass', including a memo from the Director-General. Such moments, however, are soon forgotten and this triumph was but the prelude to that period of frustration which would eventually lead to my handing in my resignation from the staff of the BBC. Shortly after Brussels there was a vacancy for a Number Two correspondent in Paris and I applied.

In earlier times BBC Foreign News had a panel of names of those staff members who had expressed an interest in being based as a correspondent abroad. Tried out in the field, as I had been, you could then be selected from the panel when a vacancy came up. Now, though, it was different. Chosen applicants had to appear before a Board. For someone like me, at that time still rather lacking in self-confidence, I found this process nerve-wracking. I gave a very low-key performance and the job went to someone else.

'Don't think being good at the job means you will get promotion,' Chris Serpell had said. Not in the BBC. The selection process was much more shifty and devious – and probably still is.

Soon I was back at Alexandra Palace, occasionally reading the main News Bulletin and also the Mid-day, quite often when Corbett Woodall had overslept and failed to make it in time. He seems to have led a rather full and exhausting social life. At least, that was my impression. His may also have been a rather large family, judging by the number of different 'nieces' he turned up with at our cricket matches. Moreover, he was absent-minded. He went home one night on the Underground and wondered why some of his fellow passengers were looking at him in a rather strange way. He had forgotten to remove his make-up! We each had our own basic make-up box. Not much more than some powder and a powder-puff if you felt the face and the nose in particular were looking a bit shiny. I don't think I ever used mine.

We also had the first, extremely basic, autocue: a very small black box placed just below the main camera lens with an operator sitting low down just to the side of it. I never had much faith in this device and usually stuck to reading the pages of the bulletin, looking up as often as possible.

My misgivings were more than justified one evening when the autocue operator arrived at the very last minute and hastily stuck the roll which carried the script into the side of the machine. I thought I noticed that she had not pushed it all the way home. Sure enough, at the very start of the bulletin, when she pressed the button to make the script roll, the whole lot shot out and fell clattering to the studio floor. No wonder I much preferred to leave reading the News to others who were much better at it, like Richard Baker, Kenneth Kendall, Robert Dougall and Michael Aspel.

It was the start of BBC 2 that eventually lifted the spirits of those of us working at Alexandra Palace and once again had me back in front of the cameras. It meant we would be running our own half-hour nightly news bulletin and writing some of it. It is much easier to read your own scripts, as you can often tell when you observe today's television newsreaders struggling to interpret what they are seeing on the large plate glass screen placed over the lens in front of them, which is the autocue.

The very first two-handed news presentation was with me and someone I much enjoyed working with, Gerald Priestland. He did the Foreign News and I did the Home News. When Gerry was away, I usually did the Foreign News and someone else took over the Home seat.

One night in November 1963 I went back into our reporters' room and picked up a very brief despatch that had just come in from Reuters on President Kennedy's visit to Dallas. Their correspondent was reporting that shots had been heard and there was evidence of blood on the side of President Kennedy's head. Gerry had gone home, so I picked up the phone and suggested that he might want to come back! That night we put on a bulletin that lasted nearly an hour. Gerry took the chair at Alexandra Palace. I went down to our studio in Broadcasting House and did a very long interview with Joseph C. Harsch, the distinguished American correspondent, based for some years in London. As we wrapped up that bulletin, still trying to come to terms with what we were reporting, I did a very lengthy review of the Fleet Street papers. Looking back, I wonder how many people actually saw that programme. In those days BBC 2 was in colour, but available only in London and the South.

3

Back Again to the Real World

In 1965 I again found myself working alongside Gerry Priestland. Like me he had decided that Television News offered too few opportunities to get out into the real world, closer to the action. On a number of occasions, when I suggested a breaking story abroad was big enough to send someone, the answer was always the same, especially while Waldo Maguire was editor: 'I would be delighted to send you, but we don't have the money.' So, when Gerry was offered the job as one of the two correspondents in Washington he gladly took it. I was by this time back in Broadcasting House working once again alongside Tom Barman as his acting, unpaid, assistant diplomatic correspondent.

In 1965 the Civil Rights movement in the United States was coming to a climax, focused in particular on Alabama. Ten years earlier in 1955 in Montgomery, the State capital, a black lady called Rosa Parks had been arrested for refusing to give up her seat to a white person on one of the city's buses. Under the city's laws, blacks also had to move if a white person wanted to sit in the same row. Leaders of the black community organised a boycott of Montgomery's buses and asked a black Baptist Minister called Martin Luther King to act as the president of their movement. It marked the growing momentum of the Civil Rights Movement which will always be associated with King's name, although the part played initially by the heroic Rosa Parks was recognised when she died in 2005. Her body was taken to Congress in Washington to lie in state.

In the fifties segregation was still widespread in the Southern States – in transport and schools, hotels and restaurants. Many states also employed various devices to deprive blacks of their right to vote. It was going to be a long and often murderous battle. Terrorists, probably members of the wretched Ku Klux Klan, bombed King's home. But the Montgomery bus boycott brought him his first success and national acclaim, not least for his insistence that the fight against racial injustice must remain non-violent, no matter what outrages were committed by those who fought against it.

Although, before he died, President Kennedy had proposed a wide ranging civil rights bill to Congress, it was his successor, President Lyndon Johnson (LBJ), who had the greatest impact in supporting the movement to 'civilise' the South. LBJ was a southerner himself, but he was also an extremely astute politician when it came to national affairs.

In 1964 the Civil Rights Act prohibited racial discrimination in public places and called for equal opportunity in employment and education. But it was the devious and dishonest methods employed in the South to stop blacks from registering to vote that brought about the most significant protest led by King. In 1965 he helped to organise a protest march in Alabama from Selma to Montgomery. Initially, the demonstrators got no further than the bridge leading out of Selma, where the local police were waiting for them and drove them back with clubs and tear gas. The dreadful pictures were shown nationwide on television and caused great shock and anger. King immediately announced that they would try again. That was when I was sent from London to help Gerry cover what looked like being – indeed was – a very dramatic story. A judge had ruled that the demonstrators had every right to march. LBJ's hand was also very much in evidence when the Alabama National Guard was put under Federal control to guarantee the demonstrators' safety.

The night before the second march was due to begin Gerry and I decided that we ought to find somewhere to stay inside Selma so that we could be with the marchers when they started, and especially to see what would happen when they reached the bridge. After a quick visit to a local branch of Sears Roebuck to buy comfortable sleeping bags we were directed by the organisers to a house where we could spend the night. I think a black family lived there, but I never met them, either then or later. A black Baptist minister shared the large living room with Gerry while I slept on the floor in the kitchen.

56

Next morning we were up at dawn and walked with the demonstrators as far as the first of their overnight stops, where they were able to set up camp. It was there, surveying the scene, that I had a moment when I felt Gerry had temporarily lost his grip. He suddenly started talking to me in a rather loud voice about cricket. Did I think we could win the current match at Lords? As I knew Gerry didn't have the faintest idea of the difference between a silly mid on, a short leg, or a gully, I was, to say the least, a bit startled. Then I understood. Turning round I saw a group of the local plain clothes police standing right beside us, led by the infamous Sheriff Jim Clark. They looked like a bunch of very unpleasant characters from a B movie. One of the leading 'creeps' was telling the sheriff in a loud voice that 'these people' did not appreciate that they were there for our 'protection'.

With an agency camera team based in the States sent to join me, I now went back to a hotel in Montgomery each night, joining the marchers early the following day. My first thought was to get an interview with Martin Luther King. The camera man was a genial and boisterous New Yorker and the sound recordist a southerner. The camera man lost no opportunity to express his robust opinion of 'the southern white trash' who were causing all these problems. During our second day on the road there was a moment when a householder came to his front door, shouting abuse and waving a gun. I can't remember exactly what the camera man said as he filmed the confrontation. Nothing I could repeat here – and nothing we could listen to again. Our southern sound recordist had removed his link to the camera and retreated to a discreet distance!

We eventually got an opportunity to talk briefly to King when he placed himself at the front of the marchers. 'Briefly' because the camera team would have to walk backwards. Holding the microphone, I allowed the front row to catch up with me and then slipped into the middle beside King.

I was promptly grabbed by the security guards but managed to blurt out to King that I was from the BBC and had come all the way from London to talk to him.

'Try that again,' he said, 'in ten minutes and we will do it.'

It was, as I said, a rather brief encounter, the camera man walking backwards holding a very heavy camera. I asked King what he hoped to do in Montgomery, pointing out that, when they reached the Governor's Mansion, Governor George Wallace had already said he would not see them.

'Oh, he'll see us all right,' said King.

How right he was! The numbers grew as we made our way along the route, thousands eventually turning up in Montgomery.

Gerry had already returned to Washington, where the daily circuits on the transatlantic cable allowed him to report on the effect the march was having on public opinion across America. Now, suddenly, my communication problems were solved. A row of telephone boxes had been set up for the Press. I simply had to call a number in White Plains, New York, to be put through on a transfer charge call to BBC News in London. For the rest of that day I was able to voice a piece in broadcast quality virtually every hour on the hour.

It is true that communication problems were less in the United States than anywhere else in the world. But 'live' from a telephone box in Alabama in the Deep South? In those days it seemed almost miraculous.

As the vast crowd began to drift away, I went to the March Headquarters in Montgomery, expecting to find them fairly jubilant. Instead, I instantly detected an air of gloom. One of the marchers, a white woman, had been driving home with some black companions when the car was ambushed by a white gunman. She had been killed instantly. Although it was in 1965 that LBJ got Congress to approve the Voting Rights Act, eliminating all the barriers that had been raised to stop Southern blacks from voting, there was still some way to go in 'civilising' the South.

My next problem was getting out of Montgomery and back to Washington. All flights from the local airport were full. I phoned Gerry to ask his advice and he suggested I went overland, either to Birmingham or New Orleans.

'Good idea, Gerry,' I said. 'I will get the train to New Orleans. Goodbye.'

I put the phone down before he could have second thoughts. It was my first visit to the city where they play my kind of music, the music we often danced to in my youth. In New Orleans you could hear it almost everywhere you went. Of the various bars I visited that evening, I particularly remember the one in which Clarence 'the Frog' Henry was seated at the piano, virtually surrounded by admirers. Since then I have been several times to New Orleans. It is one of my favourite places.

1965 was the year I first began thinking of moving on from the BBC and having more control over my life and my career. The catalyst was another illustration of the way BBC management chose to manipulate staff appointments.

Once again I had been working alongside Tom Barman in Foreign News when a decision was taken to make the job of Assistant Diplomatic Correspondent a permanent appointment. I applied as I was already doing the job. It was during one of those annual interviews that Donald Edwards, the News Editor, let slip that an Agency correspondent currently working out of Moscow would be 'a strong candidate'.

I looked at Edwards and said, 'You've told me all I need to know.' Somewhat disconcerted, he blustered and tried to tell me that no decision had been taken, that it would be up to the Board.

It was the Agency correspondent from Moscow who got the job because someone had decided he would be a useful member of staff. Despite my disappointment, I subsequently found him agreeable company.

4

My Final Years on the Staff

Despite inevitable feelings of rejection, 1965 would turn out to be not only my last year on the staff of the BBC, but also my most enjoyable working abroad as a special correspondent. One day I was told that a decision had been taken to send me to Vietnam. Hang on. Were they trying to tell me something?

Although LBJ had proved to be an immensely skilful politician in American domestic politics, he now made what turned out to be a disastrous decision in foreign affairs. He was persuaded – and 'persuaded' may be the right word – that the war in Vietnam could be won. The build up of American forces would begin.

Stopping off in Singapore, I then got a flight to Saigon on an Air Vietnam Caravelle airliner and noticed, with some understandable apprehension, that there were only three other passengers, all of them American servicemen who had probably been enjoying some R and R. Was it really going to be that grim?

Certainly there had been a ghastly incident just two days before my arrival. A device like a small land mine had exploded without warning on board a very popular floating restaurant in Saigon. Just as help was arriving to attend the dead and severely injured a second explosion mowed down a few more. So, lesson number one, passed on to all colleagues who came after us: if you hear an explosion, don't go too near until you hear the second one go off.

My first stop on arrival was the best hotel in Saigon, The Continental. Grahame Greene must have spent some time there when he was writing *The Quiet American*, if only to enjoy a glass or two in the delightful open verandah bar on the ground floor.

Far from looking like a city under siege, Saigon seemed full of vitality during daylight hours. There were good restaurants, like my personal favourite, the Arc en Ciel in the Cholon district, though it was not without a reminder to be a little wary: wire mesh covered the entrance in case anyone thought of disturbing the diners by throwing in something like a hand grenade or small bomb.

Shops were open late into the evening, as were any number of bars and cafés, many providing those 'extra services' which American servicemen in particular would be seeking out before returning to active duty somewhere in the jungle. Until 11.00 p.m. the seamier side of life in Saigon was very much in evidence. Then came the nightly curfew. In the final minutes before the hour the streets of the city were the scene of a frantic scramble; cars, taxis, pedalos, trishaws raced along in a desperate effort to beat the deadline.

Back in the sanctuary of The Continental I would sometimes take another glass at the ground floor verandah, enjoying the slightly cooler, tropical night air drifting across the open balcony.

The streets now deserted, we would then see coming across the square our own, personal 'White Mouse', which was the name we gave to the rather small, white-uniformed policeman who persuaded us it was his special duty to take care of us. Leaning out over the balcony, we often handed him down a few cigarettes, enough to keep him going until dawn when the curfew lifted.

My first, rather distant, sighting of the actual war came just a few days after my arrival. Early in the evening I crossed the square from The Continental to The Caravelle Hotel on the other side, also a popular base for visiting correspondents. The bar on the rooftop took you away from the heat and dust and noise of the city. Suddenly, on this lovely evening, the sky beyond the outskirts of the city was lit up by bursting star shells. The Americans were looking to see if the Viet Cong were making any move under cover of darkness.

They, however, were safely concealed in a network of tunnels, undetected, beneath the feet of the Americans. Some of the tunnels actually extended beneath the run-way of Saigon Airport. Today visitors to Ho Chi Minh city, as it is now called, can do what I did some 30 years later – scramble through a section of tunnel that has since been widened for easier access, leading to quite a large underground room, once the Command HQ of one of the most forward VC units.

I was partnered as a BBC special correspondent in Vietnam by another of my favourite colleagues, David Willey. He would concentrate on servicing the Radio while I would do the Television. And this time not with an Agency crew. Hang the expense! The bosses back at Alexandra Palace had finally decided to send out a team from London, led by one of the very best camera men, Peter Beggin. Until now most of the work covering Vietnam had been done by another of the BBC's greatest correspondents, Anthony Lawrence. Based in Hong Kong, Tony was the resident 'Chinawatcher'. Actually getting into China to see what was going on was very difficult in those days. Watching, listening and then interpreting was the best alternative.

Until the camera team arrived from London, David and I both went each afternoon to the daily 'briefing' by the Americans. We all called it 'The Five o'clock Follies' as they constantly tried to give us the impression that all was going wonderfully well. It was all great success – not just for the Americans but also the ARVN Forces (the Army of the Republic of Vietnam).

If one of these briefings did come up with a story worth repeating, we still had a huge problem getting a piece through to London in broadcast quality. When I first saw the studio at Saigon Radio I wondered if it were even possible to make contact beyond the city itself. All the equipment was very ancient and decrepit. Yet the Chinese woman who operated it was nothing short of a miracle worker. First, she somehow managed to make contact with Paris; then we would be 'patched through' to London. I don't think London ever said they had received our despatches 'loud and clear', but they were just good enough to put on the air, usually in *Radio Newsreel*. Afterwards, there was usually time to take a taxi down to the Arc en Ciel to celebrate.

Before I left London for Vietnam, Television News said they really wanted more pieces on how the ordinary people were being affected – how were they coping day to day; something, of course, about the build-up of American Forces, but rather less of the jungle patrols and exchanges of fire with an unseen enemy. That suited me. If I went on a jungle patrol I would want to be with a party of Gurkhas. They were outstandingly good at jungle warfare, as they had proved in Malaya and many other places. These were the days long before correspondents in war zones dressed up in military fatigues, flak jackets and tin hats to get themselves 'embedded' with a fighting military unit.

Dressed in slacks and a short-sleeved sports shirt, I did, however, take some precautions. I learnt a little Vietnamese, including this useful phrase. Phonetically it reads: 'Toy Noy Ann. Chew Kong Fie Noy Me.' 'I am English. I am not American.' Speaking French occasionally was also useful. North Vietnam's quarrel with France ended at Dien Bien Phu. Now there was no safer place in Saigon to enjoy some time off than the French Club. We managed to get temporary membership and, at the week-ends in particular, it was just like stepping back into the pre-war years when the whole region was French Indo-China, part of the French Empire.

For six weeks we were in and out of Saigon as we went to various parts of the country, right up to the demarcation line, the frontier dividing the North and the South. We had to return to Saigon at regular intervals in order to wrap up the film and take it out to the airport to be flown to London. But transport was never a problem. The Americans were always very obliging. We went everywhere by air, usually in helicopters. That 'terpocketer ... pocketer' sound of helicopter blades still lives with me.

Occasionally, they laid on a larger aircraft for an organised press outing, as when we were taken to see the huge new port development at Camranh Bay. Most memorable though was the visit we made to Hue, right up on the frontier. Here the tension seemed much greater and the atmosphere was rather creepy. We searched out the local French Club to find somewhere to stay the night and discovered we were the only visitors. There was 'alternative' accommodation – long wooden boats, covered with a canopy, floating gently in the middle of the harbour, where you could eat and sleep, with a young woman present to provide 'additional services'. Rather dangerous! And I don't mean near certainty of contracting a sexually transmitted disease – it was tempting for an active member of the Viet Cong to come alongside in the middle of the night and cut your throat. Yet I was told the boats still did a reasonable business with American servicemen.

However, we were in Hue for what turned out to be one of the most enjoyable of our adventures. The following evening we boarded a small patrol boat, manned by Vietnamese, but with an American officer in command. On the bow of the boat was a small cannon. We set off down the Perfumed River *en route* for the open sea and then down the coast to the American base at Danang. We were hunting for gun-runners, anyone suspected of supplying ammunition to the VC. Our first target was a small fishing boat returning to port. A thorough search confirmed there was nothing suspicious on board. But they did have some lovely fish – so we bought some! That evening, as we moved out to sea, the crew cooked us a delicious supper. The Vietnamese are good cooks.

Our next encounter with a suspect vessel was much more spectacular. On the horizon I saw what seemed at first like a gigantic butterfly. It was the sails of a huge junk. Our American commander had no doubts. He went straight to the cannon and fired a shot across its bows. The sails were immediately lowered and the junk came to a stop. We approached it rather cautiously, but a thorough search revealed that it was not carrying anything remotely suspicious and we sent it on its way. We continued south through the night without making any further contacts, looking forward to a very decent breakfast, as always, in the Officers' Mess at Danang.

Soon we would be back again a little further north in the Gulf of Tonkin. We were joining the Navy. I don't know if you have ever thought it might be fun to land on an aircraft carrier, but I would definitely advise against it. That was one thrill I could have done without. We were joining the USS *Bon Homme Richard*, the 'Bonnie Dick' as they often called it, a name that has lived on in the US Navy ever since the War of Independence.

Looking down as our small, twin-engined bi-plane arrived overhead, it seemed to me that the deck of the carrier was not much longer than a match-stick. From the passenger cabin you see very little as you sweep round and descend on the final approach. Then, just as you seem to be diving into the sea, you feel the bump as the wheels hit the deck, followed by what seems like an emergency stop as the hook underneath the aircraft catches one of the hawsers to stop you. The sudden jolt was severe enough to send all our camera equipment sliding down the aisle to the front of the plane.

Taking off again two days later was even more alarming. No catapult. Instead, we went right to the stern of the carrier, revved up the two propeller driven engines and made a run for it. There was a rather sickening dip as we left the bow of the carrier, but somehow we stayed airborne. Should you ever want to land on a carrier make sure you do it in a helicopter or one of those vertical take-off and landing aircraft (a truly magnificent British invention).

The US Navy made us very welcome. However, the offer of a drink to celebrate our (safe) arrival meant either coffee or something like a dozen different varieties of fruit juice. None of that 'splicing the main brace' that might have restored a near normal heart beat on a British naval vessel. The US Navy was 'dry'.

The *Bon Homme Richard* was a very busy ship. There was no need of an alarm call in the mornings as the fighter bombers began thundering off the flight deck soon after dawn. Operations went on around the clock until the evening. As one flight left another was pulled up to the launch area, ready to get away in time to leave space for the first flight to return.

I was in Vietnam for about six weeks and there are two images from those days that still live with me. The first is a shot that Peter took of three straw hats, pretty ribbon round the brims; they belonged to three petite Vietnamese schoolgirls and were hanging on pegs just inside the door to their home. We were there to talk to their mother. They knew they would not see their father again. An officer in the ARVN, he had just been killed in action somewhere in the jungle. It was astonishing when we got home to find out how many people vividly remembered seeing those three little hats when our report went out on Television News.

The other image takes me to a flight we took back to Saigon on an American DC-3. An extra passenger was laid out in the aisle between the seats – wrapped inside a black bag. A dead American soldier making his last journey home. Those two images really sum up the tragedy of the Vietnam War – for the Americans and the people of Vietnam.

One day we got back to The Continental in Saigon to find some good news. London was apparently very pleased with our efforts and invited us to take a week off in Hong Kong. We arrived in what was still our colony and booked into what seemed a rather smart hotel which had recently opened. It was called The Mandarin and still retains today the reputation of being one of the most luxurious in the world. I have no idea what it cost then for room and breakfast. Thankfully, the BBC was picking up the bill.

We enjoyed the good life for no more than three days before I got one of those brief cables: 'Proceed Delhi soonest.' India and Pakistan were again at war over Kashmir. For British audiences that was a far more important story than Vietnam.

Once again I found myself joining Ivor Jones, who was still the resident correspondent in India, and once again I was soon enjoying another great adventure up in the Himalayas. It meant that Peter and I would have to go our separate ways. He went west to the fighting. I went once more to the north-east, along with five other international journalists, including CBS, Reuters and AFP (Agence France Presse). The Indian Government was anxious to show us the frontier between Sikkim and Tibet. The Chinese were again threatening to invade India in support of their friends in Pakistan. There were accusations that India had built military posts on the Tibetan side of the frontier. It was total nonsense, but enough to alarm Delhi. So the plan was to take us there and then tell the world it was not true.

The President's own DC-3 was put at our disposal, comfortably furnished, including a bed, which was promptly grabbed by the correspondent from AFP. Our initial destination was to be Gangtok, the capital of Sikkim. From there we were taken up to the Tibetan frontier at Nathu La. Looking down into the valley from an Indian forward observation post I first saw a group of the People's Liberation Army: horse soldiers lying happily in the grass in the warm sunshine having a picnic. Then the major in charge of our expedition pointed out a small platoon of Chinese soldiers climbing the peak to our right which ran very close to the frontier. None of this was desperately threatening and certainly I saw no evidence of any Indian posts on the wrong side of the frontier. It was a very enjoyable morning out in the mountains though.

There was now only one way I could immediately get the story to London. Back in Gangtok I got off a long cable to Newscasts (the BBC cable address) describing the scene and adding that the Indian Army seemed very much better prepared and certainly better equipped than they had been in 1962. (My despatch was read in the studio as before, though I was asked to voice the whole piece when I got back to Delhi.) This time China made no attempt to cross the frontier and today, some forty years later, the pass at Nathu La, the highest between India and China is open for goods traffic between the two countries.

As the war in Kashmir came to an end I went back to London to receive a number of kindly memos from the senior management praising me for my efforts in Vietnam and India. One of them came from the Director General, Hugh Greene.

5

Look Out, World! Here I Come

Despite being sent abroad on three great stories in the past 12 months – Selma to Montgomery, Vietnam and India – 1966 began with me still wondering where my career would now take me. As so often in my life, the answer came without my having to look for it, though it would demand a fairly drastic decision.

As at the very start of my career when the history and cricket master at school got me my first job as a journalist on the local paper, cricket contacts would play some part in it. I was a member of the Bushmen.

One Sunday afternoon at a delightful fixture in Kent, near Tunbridge Wells, we were fielding and one of the opposition batsmen clipped a ball off his pads and down to the fine leg boundary. I chased after it and, just inside the boundary skilfully picked it up, turned and, in one elegant movement, hurled it back to our wicket-keeper, the Head of Television, Kenneth Adam. He may not have been the world's worst wicket-keeper, but he was certainly the worst I ever played with.

It is true the ball should have smacked into his gloves as he held them, just above the stumps, ready to run out one of the batsmen. It is also true the ball arrived rather low and at some speed. Yet, instead of bending down to take it in his gloves, he tried to let it strike his pads at an angle and from there rattle onto the stumps. Alas, he got the angle slightly wrong and the ball, instead of hitting the pads, struck him a painful blow on his exposed ankle. He was hopping up and down in pain as our fielders gathered round offering sympathy: 'Bad luck, Ken' and 'Gosh! That must have hurt'. He cast several meaningful glances at me as if it were entirely my fault.

Eventually the game began again and, as the field was changing at the end of the over, I passed close to Robert Milne-Tyte, who knew that I was still doing quite a lot of television at the time. Out of the corner of his mouth Bob quietly said: 'Have you ever thought of a career in Radio?'

I have never forgotten what most of us cruelly thought was an hilarious incident because it was Bob, then the Assistant Head of Talks and Features in World Service, who told me some time later of a new radio programme they were starting. It was to be a news, current affairs and magazine programme, with reports and features from around the world and star guests to chat 'live' in the studio. It would be on twice a day for 40 minutes, starting with a news summary.

'You are exactly the sort of presenter we are looking for,' Bob said. 'In particular, we need someone with an established background in current affairs. The producers we have at the moment are rather lacking in that department.'

The new programme was to be called *Outlook*. There was, however, one problem. I could only have the job as a freelance broadcaster, not as a member of staff, perhaps to ensure that, if anything went wrong, they could always say I was not on the staff of the BBC, merely a freelance, so there would be no problem getting rid of me. (I am sure Bob himself never thought that way.) Within a couple of days I had decided what to do. I went to see Douglas Muggeridge, the Head of World Service Talks and Features and told him I would like the job.

At first it was for only two days a week, Thursday and Friday. How would I spend the rest of my time? I decided I would post myself to Brussels and take the family with me. There was no BBC correspondent in the Belgian capital and, since our rejection by de Gaulle, very little day to day interest in the affairs of the EEC. Nevertheless, from there I could cover both Belgium and the Netherlands, and France as well if Paris ever needed an extra hand.

Foreign News thought this a brave, even useful, idea and promptly made me the official Brussels based 'stringer' – not 'the BBC correspondent' but 'a correspondent *for* the BBC'. I had recently made contact again with Paul Davies, the American camera man, and his

Belgian wife Monique. They now lived in Brussels and could find us a flat in the same modern block as housed theirs, in the Quartier d'Europe. It seemed to be working out rather well.

My basic salary would be £30 a programme, £60 per week, initially, on no more than a very short contract that had to be signed every month. When they introduced the shorter recorded version for the middle of the night £5 was added. It may not sound much but it was more than we were getting in those days as staff reporters. For me the little extra was enough for a weekly return air ticket from Brussels to London – in on Thursday morning, out again on the last Sabena Airlines flight on Friday evening. Thus I became the BBC's first European commuter by air.

There were one or two colleagues in the BBC Newsroom who said how much they envied me, but it was too late for them to do something similar. I actually handed in my notice on the day that I was, for the second time, set up at Conservative Party Headquarters to report for the all-night Election Night programme on BBC 1, presented by the great Richard Dimbleby. I got one of the big laughs of the evening when they came to Tory HQ and asked me what the mood was. (They were losing.) I told dear old 'Dimblebugs' (as we called him) that, officially, we had heard virtually no comment so far, though we had been told that the Prime Minister, Alec Douglas Home, was 'relaxing at 10 Downing Street and he is in very good form'. This produced loud guffaws in the studio. There was no mention at that stage of conceding defeat, though Harold Wilson and his wife Mary were, perhaps, already in touch with their local removal firm and deciding what furniture they would need to take with them to No. 10.

During my two years of commuting by air from Brussels I missed the first edition of the programme only once. It was the morning the fog was so thick you could not even see out of the terminal windows at Brussels Airport. As I was always on the first flight of the day to London and the last one back on Friday my fare was only £13 return, which included breakfast on the outward journey and a supper snack on the way back.

The very first edition of *Outlook* was presented by the distinguished BBC war correspondent, Bob Reid. Bob, who possessed a lovely, warm broadcasting voice, came from Bradford in Yorkshire, and was always good fun to be with. He was nothing like that extremely irritating species we call 'professional Yorkshiremen'. Bob did Mondays and Tuesdays. The Wednesday spot was taken by Colin Hamilton, the youngest member of the team, who had spent some years working in Radio in Kenya. I then wound up the week, always hoping that we might have a laugh or two and leave the listeners looking forward to having us back again on Monday.

There were those who thought the programme format could not possibly work. Traditional thinking deplored the idea of having serious current affairs mixed up with magazine material and star guests. Truly shocking! As it was, we made a start that barely stood up to the brief. The editorial direction was, to say the least, a bit limp and unimaginative. Our salvation came in the form of an excellent journalist and broadcaster who had also worked in East Africa. His name was Michael Sumner. When he took over as editor we quickly gathered momentum. Even our early critics began to like it. If a big news story broke while we were on the air we were flexible enough to drop an item or two and pursue it. Never more so than on the day the Egyptian President, Anwar Sadat, was assassinated while taking the salute at a parade in Cairo. Our guest in the studio was David Niven.

It was a Wednesday, so Colin was presenting. As usual, he started with a quick run down of some of the main items, then briefly introduced David Niven to signal that he was there, 'live' in the studio, and we would be looking forward to talking to him later. The main current affairs story of the day then followed, during which the first news came of events in Cairo.

The rest of the programme was *all* Cairo. Someone from the huge Arabic Service in Bush House was rushed into the studio to detail what had happened and to explain the background. Calls were made to bring various correspondents and other experts into the programme by phone. We managed to get the Cairo correspondent on the line. Then a news reader arrived with the latest bulletin from the newsroom. It was one of those particularly exciting events you can get in broadcasting – all action 'off the cuff'.

At the end of the programme Colin had to apologise to David

Niven, who had sat there on the other side of the table in the studio not uttering another word. He was absolutely charming about it, simply saying how much he had enjoyed being a spectator and seeing how it was done. He accepted our invitation to come back another day, which he did – lovely man.

A story I particularly remember was the one that began with those five words: 'Houston, we have a problem.' *Apollo 13*. Could the three astronauts get safely back to Earth? Would they burn up as they re-entered the Earth's atmosphere? The final tense moments were expected in the hour before we were due on the air for our second edition at 19.00 GMT. So we were told to open up the programme an hour early.

Opposite me sat one of the BBC's top science correspondents, John Newell, and on the table we had a television set so that we could watch the full coverage from American Television. In those days television was nothing like so universal as it is now. On that day, April 17th 1970, we must have had one of our biggest audiences. Millions of people around the world were glued to their radios as we gave them a minute by minute account of what we were seeing and hearing from our television screen on the studio table. Then came the terribly tense moment when *Apollo 13* entered the Earth's atmosphere. Would it burn up and disintegrate?

For a few agonising minutes – four, I think – the crew would be out of contact with Mission Control as the lunar lander, that had become their lifeboat, plunged into the Earth's atmosphere. Then, at last, we could hear them again. They were almost safe. We even saw the three parachutes open to drop the capsule fairly gently into the South Pacific near Pago Pago. Warships and helicopters were waiting close by to rush to the scene and pull *Apollo* and its crew from the water.

John and I both enjoyed the experience enormously. Then he went back to his office to do whatever he was doing before he joined me. I stayed on in the studio because it was now 19.00 GMT – time to present the edition of *Outlook* we had been planning for that day. I had another 45 minutes 'live' on the air before I could hurry down to the BBC Club bar in the basement to celebrate with a pint of draught Guinness. It may have been two!

Speaking of Guinness, I often took a glass or two between the first and second editions in the Club bar with a really great broadcaster called Sam Pollock. Several days a week Sam did our review of the Fleet Street papers. In his hands it was always an opportunity to get some laughter into the programme – as it was later with an Australian colleague, John Thompson. Sam was from Northern Ireland and had spent some years in the Enniskillen Fusiliers, otherwise known as 'The Skins'. Part of his service had been in China. He was enormously good company and, when it was known that the two of us had spent an hour or so in the Club, the team in the studio often claimed that they had, for safety's sake, put in 'the Guinness filter'.

Not, I assure you, that we ever sounded remotely the worse for wear. But I have since been told that the producers made some small edits from the first edition because it took me perhaps one and half minutes longer to get through the second!

It was Sam himself who invented the notion of a 'Guinness filter'. The name of one political figure gave him particular problems: the African leader El Haji Sir Abubaker Tafawa Balewa. One night he made a complete nonsense of it on the second edition.

'Woops!' he said, 'Someone put in the Guinness filter.'

Sam did eventually master that name but, a week later, poor old El Haji Sir Abubakar Tafawa Balewa was assassinated. Quite apart from being a great voice on World Service, Sam also did a weekly letter from London for New Zealand Broadcasting. There he became so popular the New Zealanders eventually flew him out as their guest to meet his many fans.

For about two years in Brussels I found enough work to keep me very well occupied. One of the big events was a British Week, hugely enjoyed by the Belgians, many of whom remembered the joyful scene when British troops liberated Brussels towards the end of the Second World War. The band of the Black Watch parading up and down the Grand Place brought a few tears to the eyes. It was magnificent.

As I had hoped I went down to Paris a few times to help out, and also covered the Winter Olympics in France in 1968, which turned out to be 'a nice little earner'. Foreign News in London omitted to put me on an all-embracing contract and looked with horror at the final bill, plus expenses, when they saw I had been doing seven or eight pieces a day for two weeks, getting paid for every single one.

Then came 'The Harold and George Show'. Harold Wilson, the British Prime Minister and George Brown, his Foreign Secretary, set off on a European tour to analyse our chances of joining the EEC. Christopher Serpell arrived from London and I was contracted to act as his producer, first in Belgium and then in the Netherlands and Luxembourg.

One evening in the Hague we took Peter Snow, then working for ITN, to dine with us in a restaurant specialising in Javanese *rijsttafel*, a particularly delicious feast involving a very large number of spicy dishes. Next day, Peter could hardly stop talking about how much he had enjoyed it. Frankly, there was not much to talk about as far as the mission of Harold and George was concerned. It was already fairly obvious that, much as five of the six nations wanted us, the time was not yet ripe for a second British application.

I suppose I could have stayed on in Brussels to become a spokesman for the British contingent based there, but I did not think such a life would be very exciting. So it was back to Britain and an immediate offer of work in television. I had already had a letter from Sir Geoffrey Cox, the editor, asking if I would like to join ITN. I thanked him but turned it down.

Then came an offer from an old friend and colleague to present a series of programmes on BBC 2 looking at the history of Germany from 1870 to 1970. This would introduce me to one of the most fascinating people I ever interviewed – Ernst 'Putzi' Hanfstaengl, the man who was at one time Hitler's Foreign Press Chief. (Putzi means 'tiny'. He was well over six foot tall. So that is one joke we share with the Germans.) We met at Hanfstaengl's home in Munich. He was actually born in Bavaria into one of the nation's leading and very well connected families – very much a part of Munich's 'high society'. The family wealth derived from an art business started by his grandfather and based in Munich, but eventually with branches in both London and New York.

Hanfstaengl's own links with the United States, which were to play such an important part in his life, came directly from Katherine, his mother. She was American, the daughter of a German who had fled to the United States as a political refugee in the middle of the 19th century and actually took part in the American Civil War. Hanfstaengl's earliest connection with the United States could hardly have been better. He was determined to finish his education in America and was accepted at Harvard. He soon became a rather popular figure with his fellow students, not least through his outstanding ability as a pianist. At one stage in his life he had wanted to be a professional musician. But it was the contacts and friendships he made among his fellow students at Harvard that were to prove so important for him during the Second World War. One of them was Franklin Delano Roosevelt, the future President.

Hanfstaengl was back in Munich in 1922 where he met Adolph Hitler and, like so many, was overwhelmed by his skill as an orator. He first heard him making a speech in a Munich beer hall, explaining how he would give back to the German people their dignity and self-esteem after the country had endured so much misery and poverty under the punitive reparations demanded by the Treaty of Versailles at the end of the First World War.

In one of the episodes of our BBC 2 German History programme someone told a story to illustrate the total collapse of the German mark, to the point where it became just a worthless piece of paper: two elderly ladies were on their way to the bank, pushing a wheelbarrow full to the brim with paper money. Somehow their attention was diverted. When they turned back the wheelbarrow was gone, but the thief had just dumped the money in the gutter. Apochryphal? Possibly. But it was that grim.

Ernst 'Putzi' Hanfstaengl's early role in the rise of Adolph Hitler was to introduce him to important and influential members of Munich society. He told me that so many people, like him, began to see in this man someone who might be able to do all that was needed so desperately to put the country back on its feet. Then, when the time came, someone else could take his place. In short, as Hanfstaengl told me during the interview, they could 'use' Hitler and then replace him. Too late they learned how ruthless the Nazis could be with anyone who sought to oppose them.

Listening again to my tape recording of the interview I can still picture Putzi's son, Egon, standing close to the piano where his father was seated. Once or twice I noticed Egon slightly raise his eyebrows, as if to question something his father had just said. A slight readjustment of the true facts, or merely the fading memory of a man now in his eighties? Certainly he was still able to give me a very colourful account of the 1932 election campaign that finally brought the Nazis to power the following year. Hitler flew round the country to rallies in a Junkers aircraft. Hanfstaengl went with him. He told me how brilliantly Hitler was able to manipulate vast crowds, as if conducting an orchestra: quietly at first before slowly raising the tempo and finishing with a crescendo that would bring the audience to its feet.

When he left the platform, Hitler would depart immediately. Those who came hoping to see him, shake his hand or even touch his coat were disappointed. 'He's gone,' they would be told. 'He's already flown away.' The God had descended briefly from the heavens, but was now off to win the hearts and minds of more followers.

'It was,' 'Putzi' told me with a laugh, 'just like an election campaign today in America.'

Hanfstaengl's main rôle in the campaign came at the end of the day. Hitler would be totally exhausted and wanted only to be shut away in a room with his favourite piano player, usually to listen to something by Wagner. He often asked for something from *Tristan and Isolde*, though his favourite was the overture to *Die Meistersinger*.

From being one of Hitler's closest associates in the twenties and early thirties, Hanfstaengl slowly began to feel their association was becoming weaker. His American wife, Helene, after sixteen years of marriage, decided she had had enough. His lack of consideration and constant philandering made her seek a divorce in the spring of 1936. An American citizen, she stayed on in Germany, having quickly found a much more satisfactory lover. Later, she returned to America, sick of the Nazis.

In 1937, the year after the divorce, 'Putzi' himself would have to make a much more hasty exit. Those who resented him and the influence he might have wielded over the Führer, now had every opportunity to plot against him. Joseph Goebbels and the head of the Gestapo, Himmler, were particularly keen to get rid of him. For his part 'Putzi' told me how shocked he had been by those events much earlier in the summer of 1934. Ernst Roehm was leader of the

Stormtroopers – the Brownshirts, the military wing of the Nazi Party. He wanted them to become part of the German Army, with himself in control. The Army viewed these ambitions with horror, as did many of Hitler's wealthy conservative supporters. Seeing disaster looming, Hitler resorted to murder. Roehm was killed, along with about 200 of his associates, in what came to be called 'The Night of the Long Knives'. According to Hanfstaengl it was from that moment he and many others began to realise that 'using' Hitler, then getting him to move on, was clearly no more than wishful thinking.

Putzi's relationship with the Führer was terminated in 1937. Officially, he was being sent on a mission to Spain, ostensibly to give Hitler a detailed assessment of the progress of the Spanish Civil War and to offer his advice to German correspondents working in Spain. He was more than a touch disconcerted when he was told he would be parachuted in; even more so when he discovered during the flight that they were planning to drop him over the area still held by the Republicans. It would have been a death sentence.

Fortunately, the plane developed a fault in one of the engines. After landing, while still in Germany, the pilot (who may have been helping him) said that the necessary repairs could not be carried out until the following day. Hanfstaengl took the opportunity to escape into Switzerland, where he was later joined by his son, Egon, before the two of them moved on to London. Egon's final school years were at St Paul's Boys' School in West London, before he went off to the States to join his mother. Once there, Egon found his own place at Harvard.

This is where the story takes an incredible twist. At the outbreak of the Second World War Hanfstaengl, supposedly marked out as a dangerous Nazi, was sent to an internment camp at Clacton in Essex. Subsequently, he was among those internees shipped across the Atlantic to camps in Canada. There an old friend, and close associate of Roosevelt, discovered him and persuaded the President that the fellow student he had known at Harvard was much too valuable to be locked away in Canada. He should be brought to Washington and set up to analyse events in Germany, particularly through listening to Berlin Radio. Initially, the British, particularly Churchill, were far from keen to release him. Eventually, however, a deal was made and he found himself established in a pleasant house just outside Washington. But Churchill insisted someone be in the house to keep an eye on him: a permanent guard. The job was given to a young army sergeant who had volunteered for the American Forces some time before America got drawn into the war by Pearl Harbor. His name was Egon Hanfstaengl! So for some time father and son worked together, collecting and analysing information for the benefit of the American Intelligence Services.

Looking back now on the hour or so I spent chatting to Ernst Hanfstaengl at his home in Munich I have two other memories. One is hearing Egon say that, when he was very young, he thought Adolf was one of the best and kindest uncles a boy could ever have, always ready to give him some of his time. The other is Hanfstaegl's summing up of the monster he helped to power.

'Hitler compared himself,' he said, 'to Frederick the Great. In fact, he was just Adolf the Only.'

During the early years working for *Outlook*, certainly once I returned from Belgium, there was more than one opportunity to think again about my decision virtually to turn my back on domestic radio and television and base my career in BBC World Service.

Stephen Bonarjee for whom I had worked at Alexandra Palace, initially presenting that nightly regional news magazine *Town and Around*, told me that I had made a very bad career move. He seemed to look on going to Bush House as little better than self-imposed exile. Steve was now the head of the two leading current affairs programmes: *Ten O'Clock* and the *Today* programme with it's very popular presenter, Jack de Manio. Once or twice when Jack was away, I had been called in to take his place for a week or so. Other stand-ins included Des Lynham, Barry Norman and John Timpson. John eventually achieved his long held ambition to get the job permanently.

In the summer of 1969 Steve signed me up for a month. The daily shift usually began about six o'clock. The overnight producer set up the whole programme, writing all the scripts and suggesting a list of questions for any interviews. On this particular morning I was driving into London and turned on my car radio to check on the overnight news. I was a bit shaken to hear that tanks from the Soviet Union and other Warsaw Pact countries had suddenly arrived in

Prague to crush an attempt by Czechoslovakia (as it then was) to seek independence and freedom. They had been calling it 'the Prague Spring'. It looked like being a rather busy morning!

In the first edition I did what was, at that stage, the longest interview they had ever had at the top of the *Today* programme – five or six minutes. The producer had to leave it all to me to pursue the relevant questions. And where did he go to find someone with the expertise to analyse these dramatic events? Why, Bush House of course, and the Czech Section.

After a month working for *Today* Steve Bonarjee again tried to entice me to give up Bush House and join his team, promising me a healthy contract. I assume it would have meant presenting and reporting and, possibly, the occasional assignment abroad. But I felt my loyalty belonged to *Outlook* and BBC World Service. It was domestic radio that seemed like a rather backward step. *Outlook* had become increasingly popular, enjoying huge audiences worldwide. Moreover, I particularly enjoyed the atmosphere in Bush House. It was a bit like a branch of the United Nations, with broadcasters and producers from all over the world to support more than thirty different language services. While World Service in English was broadcast around the clock, the language services were sensibly timed to go out when their audience was awake, which often meant during the night, GMT.

There was, for example, a very big audience on the other side of the world in China, listening in Mandarin, Cantonese and English. The most dramatic proof of that came during the huge demonstrations in Tianamnen Square in Beijing in 1989, when two students were seen carrying a big banner which simply said: 'Thank You BBC'.

We always knew that in many parts of the world people tuned in to find out what was actually going on in their own countries. There is a famous story of President Kenneth Kaunda of Zambia, hosting an international conference and suggesting a brief adjournment while they all listened to BBC World Service News.

At one time the Soviet Union was so alarmed by the influence of the BBC they spent more money trying to jam (block out) our broadcasts than we were spending putting all the programmes together. Yet millions of listeners in the Soviet Bloc still heard us regularly. In the end there was one other very important factor that persuaded me to base my career in Bush House. It is summed up by something that happened when Michael Kaye, a good friend, was doing a stint as *Outlook*'s editor. I had almost finished the script for the day when I discovered there was an additional item I had not been told about. Michael came to my desk and, pacing about in front of me, said: 'Oh, don't worry. All you need to say is...' Before he could finish I interrupted him with a mild reprimand: 'Michael ... (slight pause) ... I do the words.' It is a story Michael often told with some relish to the students he has taught in some of the essentials of broadcasting techniques.

'Doing the words'? – your own words – is an essential part of being a broadcaster on Radio, where you have to have a personality as well as a voice. This is certainly true when you are presenting a programme week in week out, as I did, for more than thirty years as one of the founders of *Outlook*. Radio is, in reality, a very intimate technique. Sitting alone in the studio facing the microphone, it doesn't really matter how many millions of listeners you have (in our case an average of 30 million) each one should somehow feel you are talking only to them – a bit like phoning an old friend and saying, 'You'll never guess what's happened now...'

That is one of the reasons why I never had the least desire to go back to Television News, even though yet another attempt would be made in the early eighties to lure me away from World Service. Spending much of your career trying to read someone else's, sometimes ill-written words, off a plate glass screen in front of the camera is not my idea of a good time. Moreover, *Outlook* was already giving me wonderful opportunities to see even more of the world than I would have done as a staff correspondent for BBC Foreign News. Added to that was the growing list of great personalities we were able to persuade to join us 'live' in the studio for the first edition of the programme at 14.00 GMT.

Some came to talk about their newly published book. Others to enjoy the opportunity of getting in some mention of their latest film or current appearance on the West End stage. One of the first guests was the Hollywood star, Shirley MacLaine. I invited her to come and sit with me in the studio five or ten minutes before we were due to go on the air, so that I could explain what was in that day's programme. I told her I would first of all do some headlines and then introduce her, so that everyone knew she was with me. After that I told her we would have a six minute recorded interview I had done earlier, looking at one of the main news events of the day, then go back to her.

'But I don't know anything about that,' she said. 'I am not an expert in current affairs.'

'No,' I said. 'You are only here to talk about you – films, Hollywood, and your travels around the world.'

It is not quite true that she had absolutely no knowledge of current affairs. She had close access if she so desired to the intimate details of Australian foreign policy through her friendship with the then Australian Foreign Minister. But I am not one to gossip!

One memorable guest was that gorgeous woman born in 1921 in Minnesota, Ernestine Jane Geraldine Russell, the film star Jane Russell. She was in London to rendezvous with a child. Unable to have children herself, she had started her own adoptive agency in America. Some claim she was never given full credit for her talent as an actress. It was that stupendous 38-inch bust that gave her lasting fame, not only on the screen but in the 1970s with the advertisements she 'fronted' (I think that's the appropriate word) for the Playtex 'Cross Your Heart' bra, for the woman with the fuller figure. She was, not unnaturally, the victim of many vulgar jokes. Bob Hope, who starred with her in *The Outlaw*, once introduced her to an audience as 'the two and only Jane Russell'. I remember her as someone endearingly modest and genuine. So a warm 'thank you' to Jane for coming to visit us. And thanks also to 'Hot Lips', the actress Loretta Swit, who played Major Margaret Houlihan in *M*A*S*H* – one of my favourite comedy series, set in 1953 during the Korean War. Loretta Swit's parents were Polish immigrants who settled in New Jersey.

The fun and the challenge of 'live' broadcasting is coping with the unexpected, or throwing out something you have rehearsed in favour of something else – maybe an important news flash that has just come in – as happened to me on the day I told the world that someone had just shot the Pope. Action stations! Get someone up from Rome. Anyone who can fill in the details, show the reaction on the spot. Re-shape the programme as we go along. You need a very good team for that – editor, producers and studio managers – which we always had. Many is the time after a particularly 'hairy' programme we all left the studio together, heading for the BBC Club bar in the basement saying, with triumphant smiles, 'Well, that's another one we walked away from.'

Not long after we became 'airborne' on that first Monday in July 1966 we began to take the programme out of studio on a regular basis, initially to focus an edition on various parts of the British Isles. Then we became more ambitious, finding the money to travel abroad. Over the years I did virtually all the *Outlook*s from abroad, allowing me to present the programme from every continent except Antarctica.

One of our earliest 'away days' in Britain took me back to the city I have always regarded as my home. Although I was actually born in King's College Hospital in London, I spent my teenage years and early working life in Bristol, until I moved to London in 1956. The Bristol programme gave me the chance to dismiss once again the idea that someone called Christopher Columbus discovered America. If you walk up Park Street from the city centre you come to Whiteladies Road and then Blackboy Hill. That is a reminder of one of the most disgraceful episodes in Bristol's history: the city's huge and immensely profitable involvement in the slave trade. If, on the other hand, you enter the city from the M4 motorway, and then the M32, you will find yourself in Newfoundland Road. This a reminder that, in 1497, an Italian merchant adventurer called John Cabot and eighteen Bristol seamen on board a small barque called *The Matthew*, set off down the River Avon to sail on what would prove to be an historic journey. Some 35 days later they had crossed the Atlantic to land on the north east coast of the mainland of North America. This was truly New Found Land. Cabot and his crew have a far greater claim to have discovered America than Christopher Columbus, who had merely sailed into the islands of the Caribbean. Both men, however, thought they had arrived in Asia. Not that Bristol itself has many reminders of this historic voyage, apart from the statue opposite the SS *Great Britain* and the Cabot Tower overlooking the Clifton Suspension Bridge. Isambard Kingdom Brunel, who built this beautiful bridge high above the Avon gorge, is much more celebrated and remembered in Bristol than Cabot and those eighteen Bristol seamen.

Brunel's iron ship, the SS *Great Britain*, is now a huge attraction in the city docks. It was brought back as a wreck from the Falkland Islands and lovingly restored. There is also Brunel's association with Temple Meads station and the Great Western Railway from London to Bristol.

At the end of the seventies I began what would be my last appearance on television. I received a phone call from an old friend and colleague from our days with Television News at Alexandra Palace. Colin Riach was a science correspondent and had now become the producer of a very popular programme called *Young Scientist of the Year*. It was an annual competition for schools all over the country. They would come forward with various research programmes they had themselves created. It was a knock-out competition, building up to a grand finale, when one group would be declared the Young Scientists of the Year. Colin suddenly said to me: 'How would you like to present it?'

Remembering my rather dismal record at school, particularly in chemistry, I immediately said: 'Colin, I really don't know much about Science.'

With barely a pause, Colin replied: 'Excellent. You'll be perfect.' Fortunately, I was never left in the studio alone to ask intelligent questions. We always had a team of experts, led by Sir George Porter, to make the judgements. I must say I had great admiration for some of the children who took part in the series in the three years I presented it. The programme only came to an end when, very sadly, Colin died and no-one was allocated to take his place. As a result, preparations for the competition in the following year never got under way, and before anyone discovered the error it was too late. You would think with all the meetings that take place in the BBC on a daily basis someone might have noticed. Though on reflection, perhaps not!

It was that final series which earned me a rave review from Alan Hart, then Controller of BBC 1: 'I very much enjoyed this year's series which was extremely well presented. John Tidmarsh seems to look younger and get better with every passing year.' Incidentally, Alan Hart's kindly comments were not addressed directly to me or even copied to me. Contracts advised Colin not to let me see it. They thought I would only be demanding more money.

Top: The four Tidmarsh brothers back from World War I with their mother and father. Left to right: Bertie, Sidney, Jimmy and Charles, my father, the eldest of four.

Right: Early signs of leadership qualities! Worcester Park in Surrey, circa 1937, a 'Sixer' in the Cubs.

Top left: Pat in Bristol in the fifties as a member of the Rapier Players.

Top right: Reading the main television news at Alexandra Palace in the early sixties.

Bottom: Anthony Grey, the Prisoner of Peking, comes to thank Outlook for all our efforts to get him released. Left to right: Colin, Tony, Sam Pollock and me.

Top left: Goonhilly Downs, Cornwall – sending World Service out across the world.

Top right: John McCarthy joining me for *Outlook*'s 30th anniversary celebrations.

Right: In front of Bush House, the world's number one radio station.

Top: The Pass at Nathu La, the highest in the Himalayas, dividing India from Tibet. The year, 1965 during the second war between India and Pakistan. Would the Chinese invade again, as they did in 1962 through Taweng? Answer… not this time.

Bottom: Vietnam War; onboard 'The Bonnie Dick' (the USS carrier *Bon Homme Richard*) in the Gulf of Tonkin, with Peter Beggin, one of the best cameramen from BBC Television News.

COOKHAM RURAL DISTRICT COUNCIL

Oakley Green and Fifield By-election

VOTE

TIDMARSH | X

JANUARY 19th, 1965
BRAYWOOD MEMORIAL HALL, FIFIELD ROAD

Printed by Baylis & Co. (The Maidenhead Advertiser) Ltd., 80-82 Queen Street, Maidenhead. Published by Marion Walton, 76 Alexandra Road, Windsor.

Top: Just outside Honolulu, about to fly the last segment of the route the Japanese took on their way to Pearl Harbor.

Bottom left: Halfway up the Khyber on the way to the frontier with Afghanistan.

Bottom right: Pat makes a successful foray into local politics for the Liberal Party in the midsixties, a year before we move to Belgium.

Top: The original *Outlook* team, July 4th 1966. Left to right: Colin Hamilton, me, the ex-war correspondent Bob Reid and Sam Pollock.

Bottom: Terry Waite at Bush House to say how much he and his fellow Beirut hostages owed to *Outlook* for keeping them well informed, entertained and hopeful for the future.

Top: My favourite Prime Minister. Paul Eddington was working in Bristol when I first met him. He was starring with my wife Pat in a BBC TV production of *Yellow Sands*.

Bottom: The all-night General Election programme, chaired once again by me in 1983. Anne Lount, our technical assistant, along with Norman Hunt (Lab.) and Esmond Wright (Con.).

Top: David Montgomery and Manfred Rommel. The sons of the two World War II generals who became friends.

Bottom: Princess Margaret, a World Service fan, chatting to me in the *Outlook* studio during one of her visits to Bush House.

Alan Hart himself followed this up by sending someone to have a drink with me in the Bush House Club. It was an invitation to do more television, presenting *Songs of Praise*. I turned it down. It could have compromised my work for *Outlook* in the second half of each week. Supposing I was needed at the week-end to hop on a plane for some exciting destination to prepare one of the growing number of *Outlooks* from abroad. Furthermore, my week-ends were for keeping fit – cricket for the Bushmen in the summer and soccer in the winter. I was still playing soccer in my sixties, though it was what one might call a more leisurely, thoughtful kind of game. How I miss it as I have got older! Golf is no substitute.

My main reason, however, was the feeling that, even though I had been a choirboy many years ago, my personal faith could no longer be expressed in organised religion. I was certainly baptised in the Church of England, although I have never seen any photographs to prove it. (It was obviously in the days before Mother bought her first Kodak Brownie box camera.) But I have never been a regular churchgoer. So much of what the Church still teaches about those events in the Middle East more than two thousand years ago simply doesn't stand up to our understanding of the world in which we now live. In relation to the rest of the universe I once heard the Earth described as 'no larger than a single grain of sand in the Sahara Desert'.

Organised religion has certainly given us some wonderful music. It has also created some outstanding buildings. Two of my favourites are in eastern England: the cathedrals of Ely and Lincoln. If you approach Lincoln at twilight when the cathedral has been floodlit it seems suspended in the air above the city – a magical sight.

I suspect many of the steadily growing number of non-churchgoers, like me, accept that we need to find some internal inspiration as a guide to the way we live our lives. But we can do that without turning up every Sunday to hear some of the myths and miracles of two thousand years ago being re-cycled. Who are we and why are we here? These are the great unanswered questions. As I have grown older, I have come to believe that death will be the last great adventure. And if I should turn up at the Pearly Gates, I am afraid St Peter will take one look at my CV and ask me to move on.

My refusal to do *Songs of Praise* marked the end of my career in television. Do I regret it? Not for a moment. As I look now at some of the great adventures I had with *Outlook* over the years you will understand why.

Although we were initially classified as a News and Current Affairs programme, the News summary at the start of the hour, with a visit from one of the announcers, was no longer part of the programme. It came instead from the Continuity studio just before we started.

The emphasis was still on current affairs. We could still catch up with breaking news if it happened during the programme. In that event, the second edition, which was now going out as a recording, would have to be re-worked. Something of the sort happened on the afternoon that someone from the Newsroom shot into the studio with a single sheet of paper containing that news flash from Rome.

I looked at it, barely able to believe it, and then told the world: 'The Pope has been shot in Rome. His condition is not yet known.'

Once established with that very large and very loyal audience, we began to look to more distant horizons. One of our earliest excursions took us across the North Atlantic in the wake of Cabot and the Bristol seamen, bound for Newfoundland and Labrador. Our journey was a little quicker than the voyage of *The Matthew* in 1497.

We were guests of the RAF stationed in Goose Bay. From there those rather evil looking V bombers practised their navigational skills, making low level runs across the Arctic tundra in readiness for the day when they might have to seek out targets in the Soviet Union, flying across a similar landscape.

The station was also a centre for survival training. What do you do if you bail out or make a crash landing in a region where temperatures are often 30 degrees or more below zero? We set off one morning with several members of aircrew to find out. Some miles from base the NCO in charge of the exercise informed us that this was the very spot where we had come down. We had been extremely lucky to survive and, if our good luck was to continue, we had better get busy building a fire and a temporary shelter from the available brushwood. I gather we did quite well and, thankfully, were not required to spend the night in the open. We were back in Goose Bay in time for dinner in the Officers' Mess.

Only one creature I saw clearly enjoyed being out of doors at night in that climate. It was the pet Husky of the manager who ran a small radio station. When we called round at his house one evening for a drink, this beautiful hound was sitting outside on the porch. It was too hot inside for his liking.

Early in 1976 I was back again in Canada with *Outlook*. We were taking a look at Montreal and the growing misgivings of many of its citizens over the cost of staging the summer Olympics during the last two weeks in July. Mayor Jean Drapeau had been constantly reassuring everyone that the Games would pay for themselves. But his extremely ambitious plans, which included a spectacular main stadium, with a roof that was supposed to open and close, would eventually leave the city paying off debts totalling one billion dollars.

The work on the roof was not completed and one night, during a heavy downpour, the Olympic flame was extinguished. The story is that someone re-lit it with a cigarette lighter, though a genuine stand-by flame was eventually used. Apart from the debts, one other misfortune left not only Montreal but the whole of Canada less than jubilant about staging the Games. Canada did not win a single Gold Medal.

Goose Bay, Montreal and subsequent assignments in Quebec, Toronto, twice more in Montreal and right across to the Pacific coast and the glorious city of Vancouver, left me with a lasting feeling that I would have been very happy to live in Canada. I actually considered buying a property on Vancouver Island, but I could not afford it at the time. What an investment it could have been!

I was back in Vancouver in 1986 for the World Fair, celebrating the arrival on the Pacific Coast of the Canadian Pacific Railway one hundred years earlier. I woke up one sunny morning to enjoy the wonderful view to the east of the mountains cascading down from the Rockies. Why was this lovely city not named after one of my great heroes, Capt. James Cook, rather than the fifteen-year-old midshipman, who sailed with him on his second Pacific voyage and again later as a senior officer commanding one of the ships in Cook's fleet, George Vancouver from Kings Lynn in Norfolk? It is a name not nearly so universally celebrated as Cook's, except in British Columbia. But it was from his captain that Vancouver learnt his great skills as a navigator and cartographer.

On the third Pacific voyage in the late 18th century, Cook's expedition was seeking a North West Passage, linking the Pacific to the Atlantic across the top of North America. During this voyage they discovered the Pacific island which Cook named Christmas Island. Five days out from Hawaii they sighted the west coast of North America in the region of Oregon and started to work their way north. But Cook's ship, *The Resolution*, was now in a very poor state and leaking badly, so he put into Nootka for repairs, believing that he was on the main coast of Canada. He wasn't. Nootka is on the huge and enormously beautiful Vancouver Island that shields a large proportion of the mainland coast of British Columbia from the Pacific Ocean. Some accounts suggest that Vancouver, on the sister ship *Discovery*, already suspected they were on an island; eleven years later he was back there to prove it, this time commanding the expedition.

If you take the delightful ferry journey from Vancouver to Victoria, the capital of British Columbia on the southern tip of Vancouver Island, you will see the difficulties George Vancouver faced in trying to prove he was right. A number of close-knit islands in the Georgia Strait made him decide the job could only be done with small boats. As today's ferry gets close to Victoria and winds its way through Active Pass, you can see how Vancouver and his team must have envied all the Bald Eagles flying above this region, with their aerial view of the negotiable passages. Eventually, he was able to prove that the island which takes his name shields the mainland. It is a pity this brilliant seaman is not more widely recognised outside British Columbia. If you are ever in Vancouver, don't forget to pay your respects. His statue stands outside City Hall.

It was here I heard what struck me as a unique Saturday morning radio programme. In Britain we have our daily weather forecasts. In Vancouver they have 'the fishing forecast' – where to look for the fish, what bait they currently seem to be taking, etc. For fishermen, British Columbia is about as close to Paradise as you can possibly be. I saw a recent statistic suggesting that some nine million fish are caught each year in the freshwater rivers, lakes and streams, including the very popular rainbow trout. But for me salmon would be the big attraction. Never mind catching them; eating them is what I enjoy. There are no fewer than five different species indigenous to the waters of British Columbia: Chinook, Coho, Sockeye (my favourite), Pink and Chum.

One of the presenters of the fishing programme told me the story of how God created the world, according to the people who live in British Columbia. On the first day he was moving in a westerly direction across the Pacific, taking in the Far East, South East Asia, a side trip to Australasia followed by the Indian sub-continent. He then went across Africa, the Middle East, Europe, and across the Atlantic to North and South America. On the sixth day he arrived on the west coast of the Pacific and what we now know as British Columbia. At the end of that day he looked at what he had just done and said to himself: 'That is so beautiful I will never do anything better than that, so tomorrow I think I will take the day off.' No doubt he went fishing.

In the early days I had always enjoyed the moment when the newsreaders actually came to join me in the studio with a brief summary at the top of the programme. They were splendid people: Peter King, Brian Empringham, John Wing and John Stone, whose pronunciation of even the most complicated names of people and places around the world was never less than immaculate. Now, as I mentioned earlier, the news was read from Continuity, elsewhere in the building, before handing over to me. Yet we remained closely involved in some of the most dramatic and historic events in the second half of the 20th century – and never more so than in the eighties.

In October 1986 I was sent to Iceland with one of my favourite producers, Anne Theroux. We were there to do a scene-setter for the arrival of President Reagan and the Soviet leader, Mikhail Gorbachev. They were coming to prepare a treaty on the reduction of nuclear weapons. Their meeting was also an opportunity for us to take a look at a country that very rarely makes the world headlines, a country of mountains, volcanoes, thermal pools, geysers spurting out scalding hot water at regular intervals and, in many places, a landscape of black lava.

At times you feel that you are looking at the very recent creation of our world, a place God missed out during those six days on his way to British Columbia, a land that emerged later as an afterthought, bubbling up from volcanic activity on the ocean floor. In the sixties we saw how Iceland came into being as a later addition to Europe when an island, now called Surtsey, some thirty miles from the mainland of Iceland, began to appear from the sea in exactly the same way.

As for the summit meeting, it all went horribly wrong when Reagan refused to give up the plan for what was called 'Star Wars', a system that was supposed to intercept and destroy nuclear missiles while they were still out in space. He offered to share the research with the Soviet Union, but Gorbachev rejected it and went back to Moscow feeling he had been very badly let down, considering his evident willingness to make substantial progress on the main issue of reducing nuclear weapons.

So Iceland did not enter the history books as the place which saw a huge step forward in ending the Cold War. The focus of attention and the headlines didn't even last as long as those for the much earlier Cod War, when Icelanders decided to broaden their coastal limits to protect the fishing industry on which the country relies too heavily. That greatly annoyed Britain, the United States and NATO. The problem was eventually solved when a delegation representing Iceland's fishermen came to London for a meeting at No. 10 Downing Street.

The meeting was held in the Cabinet room and lured inside, for the first time anyone could remember, one of the most distinguished residents of No. 10, Humphrey the cat, checking, no doubt, to see if they had brought him a peace offering – perhaps something the fishmongers used to call 'pussie's pieces'.

The Reagan-Gorbachev meeting in Reykjavik no doubt gave Iceland's tourist industry a bit of a boost, even though it did little to suggest the world was becoming a safer place. Indeed, when George Schultz, the American Secretary of State, spoke to the Press just before leaving for home, he was very gloomy about the immediate future. Yet 'you can call me Ron' and 'you can call me Mikhail' were soon together again, this time in Washington, ready to agree a treaty designed to eliminate intermediate and short range missiles.

I was asked to go to Washington to put together an edition of *Outlook* covering this historic event. Yet I thought Washington, besieged by the world's media, was not the right place to be. In next to no time we would be interviewing each other! Then I came up with one of my better ideas: use the Washington meeting as 'cue material' and go instead to one of the Northern States, where the local inhabitants lived among the deep silos concealing America's long range, multiple warhead MX missiles. What view would they now take of the future? How did they feel living virtually in the front line of what would truly be a 'war to end all wars' because it would destroy our planet and wipe out most of the earth's population?

My choice for our base was Cheyenne in Wyoming. It is a place I had always wanted to visit, famous from all those Westerns I so much enjoyed. A few miles over the hill is Laramie. 'The Man from Laramie', starring James Stewart, is one of my favourite classic Westerns.

We checked into the delightful Hitching Post Inn from where you could hear the distant, rather soulful hooters of huge freight trains, making their way west towards Oregon. I am told if you fly over this region you can still see evidence of a much more dangerous journey taken many years earlier by those heroic families who crossed America in search of a better life in the West. Looking down from above you can still clearly see the tracks of their waggon wheels. The Oregon Trail.

Our first problem was how to get to see the missile silos and meet the people who would be responsible for firing them. We found the men at the nearby US Airforce base extremely helpful. They liked to call themselves 'The Peacekeepers', with some justification.

We were allowed to see inside one of the underground bunkers which were individually the control points for a whole area of missiles. To operate the system, two men would have to be on duty, waiting for the order to fire. They would be seated some distance apart because the system would only become operational if they *simultaneously* pressed one of the buttons on the control panels in front of them. One man could never reach out far enough to touch the critical button on *both* panels.

Next we went to see one of the places where these hideous weapons lay concealed. We set out to visit a ranch some miles out of Cheyenne. The owner was waiting for us and invited us into his house, but I was very curious to take a look at what might have been mistaken for a huge tennis court, not much more than 100 yards from his back door. It was protected on all four sides by a high wire fence. At one end was a large, round, concrete cover; some rail lines led away to the other end of the 'court'. Concealed beneath the cover, the rancher told us, was an MX missile. If the moment ever came, the concrete cover would be rolled back along the lines, opening the way for the missile to take off. The whole area was out of bounds to everyone, including the rancher, but maintenance engineers from the nearby Airforce base would come at regular intervals to make sure everything was in working order.

What a monster to have concealed virtually in your back garden! I asked him how he and his neighbours felt living so close. Weren't they rather nervous and apprehensive?

'Not really,' he said. 'They are not going to target us. After all, by the time their missiles could get here ours would already be gone.'

In the event of all-out nuclear war Wyoming could be one of the safer places to be – if only briefly.

I was soon able to see much more of this part of America, the northern States bordering Canada. *Outlook's* audience was about to enjoy a further boost. A collaboration had begun between World Service and National Public Radio in the United States. The Americans particularly enjoyed *Outlook*, so we were taken off satellite and rebroadcast five days a week right across America from WBUR in Boston to KALW in San Francisco and on up to Wrangell in Alaska.

I was sent more than once to visit some of these stations, flying the flag for World Service as well as *Outlook*. In Wrangell I was once persuaded to surprise, if not startle, the listeners, by going on the air at lunchtime to read the news headlines. Don't ask me what they were. I have long forgotten. Had I been asked to do the same thing when I was later visiting Des Moines I am fairly certain they would have started with the very latest 'Hog Prices'. There is no more important news than those little old hog prices. Years earlier they might have taken second place to the exploits in the state of those notorious bank robbers, the James Gang.

These PR visits also gave me the opportunity to put together some features for *Outlook*. One was a visit to see some of those enchanting

Bridges of Madison County, including the birthplace of that world famous American, Marion Morrison – better known as John Wayne.

We made a whole edition of *Outlook* in Detroit, a city brought to its knees by terrible riots in 1967. In four days more than 40 people died after the Police had raided an unlicensed bar. The violence was so widespread the National Guard had to be called in. White citizens fled to the suburbs as the heart of the city was torn apart. I arrived from the airport late in the evening. In the eerie semi-darkness, because of so little street lighting, I was shocked to see the devastation. Buildings were wrecked and abandoned while in several acres of the centre virtually nothing had been left standing.

This was Motown, famous as the centre of America's motor car industry and also for the Motown Music of the sixties – Diana Ross, Stevie Wonder, the Jacksons, Smokey Robinson and Martha Reeves. Martha was still living in Detroit. We were quickly introduced to Focus Hope, an organisation working for the re-integration of society, but still, fifteen years after the riots, dealing with the more urgent problem of saving many families from hunger. Feeding stations issued a monthly supply of free food, focusing particularly on mothers, children and the elderly.

I was told that in one month nearly 90,000 people, white as well as black, had visited one or other of the feeding stations. Yet there were signs that the city was coming back to life again, not least the impressive glass towers of the multi-storey hotel and commercial centre on the waterfront, aptly called The Renaissance.

In the twenties and thirties Detroit was one of America's leading entertainment centres, possessing more than 80 movie palaces, vaudeville houses and newsreel theatres. The greatest movie palace of them all, right in the centre of the city, could in its hey-day seat an audience of more than four thousand. This internally derelict building, was being lovingly restored and turned into an opera house. The acoustics inside the auditorium were certainly sensational, and wonderfully demonstrated for us by the opera singer Ara Berberian. Workmen stopped what they were doing to listen to a quiet, almost whispered passage from *The Barber of Seville*, and gave him a huge round of applause at the end. I left hoping that Detroit would deal as sympathetically with some of its other historic buildings, especially the gorgeous examples of early American vertical.

A report I read 40 years after the riots said they were now ancient history. Huge private and public investment had been poured in to develop downtown Detroit. I don't know if they were actually 'Dancing in the Street' to Martha Reeves and the Vandellas, but she became a city councillor. Since then, however, it all seems to have gone downhill. The 21st century has seen huge problems in the motor car industry and many people in Detroit are now looking for a better life elsewhere.

The nineties also gave me the opportunity to visit South America for the first time. We were asked to cover the Earth Summit in Rio de Janeiro. But how? Once again this was something we had to think about if we were putting together more than one programme. There was no point in staying in Rio, even though I was booked into a very smart hotel overlooking Copacabana Beach. The conference itself was already predicted to produce enough hot air to damage the environment even further, the very problem it was supposed to be tackling. We decided to look at Brazil itself, a country facing so many of the disasters on the Earth Summit's agenda.

I remember looking one day into the river in a town south of Sao Paulo. It was black in colour and had literally died, so full of pollution it seemed unable to move. I suspect if you fell in they would not bother to pull you out, even if they found you, as they would expect you to be already fatally poisoned. Nevertheless, a new housing development was already being built, which would move some of the local citizens away from the appalling squalor of the district where they had lived for so long and introduce them to some 20th century amenities, like clean water supply and sanitation.

As for Rio, it is not a city I am keen to visit again. Its reputation as a rather dangerous place was emphasised by the number of soldiers and armed police on duty, day and night, at regular intervals along the famous sea front and outside the hotels where most of the delegates and the media were staying.

Rio is famous for its annual carnival, but take a look behind all that glamour and you will see, climbing up behind the city centre, the mountain of squalid slums or *favellas*, home to some three million people. It would test the skills of even our slickest British estate agents to get a good price when any of these ghastly hovels changed hands as apparently they do. 'Needing some refurbishment, but located in tight knit community, enjoying fabulous views over the city to the beach. Early viewing recommended.'

It was in Rio that we chose to look at what was being done for homeless children, the 'street children'. Efforts were being made to help them. Giving them somewhere safe to stay at night was essential otherwise they could easily fall victim to the self-appointed 'death-squads', who had their own murderous methods of 'tidying up' the city streets.

However, one part of Brazil I would gladly return to if I got the chance: the Amazon rainforest. If we cannot save it from destruction the death of our planet is almost certain. Yet since the Earth Summit vast areas have been cut down. Occasionally, we get a reminder of this, as when illegal loggers murdered a nun who had been campaigning to stop them.

The Amazon was the highlight of our stay in Brazil. We made our base in Manaus, where we met someone who was one of our regular listeners, when at home in Switzerland – 007 himself, Roger Moore. On this occasion he was not carrying out an assignment for 'M'. He was there in his role as a UNICEF ambassador. We met in just about the last building you would expect to find in the middle of the Amazon rainforest – the enchanting Manaus Opera House, with its golden dome, and frontage reminiscent of Covent Garden. It was built by Europeans, over a period of fifteen years, towards the end of the 19th century.

One piece of advice. If you decide, as three of us did, to be a bit more adventurous and take a trip further into the undisturbed rainforest, watch out for howler monkeys. They don't take kindly to visitors and can be very aggressive. We could hear one large colony chattering away at nightfall and wisely decided to stay out in the river.

Back at base, as it got really dark, those who had stayed behind in our large river cruiser, where we planned to spend the night, were becoming anxious, straining to hear the sound of the outboard engine driving our small utility boat. We were travelling at some speed and I thought how unfortunate it would be if we struck some solid object floating on the surface of the river and promptly sank. How long does it take a bunch of those flesh-eating piranha fish to devour a human being? They are, I understand, voracious. Against these fears

I set the memory of how a wonderfully clear, but moonless, night was lit up for us by tens of thousands of fireflies flitting along the river bank. Sheer magic!

Some years after the Earth Summit, I was reading how one city in Brazil had managed to become something of an inspiration to other parts of the world. It was a report by a delegation from Chicago on a visit they made to Curitiba, south of Sao Paulo. Modern architecture combined with a policy of renovating the best of the older buildings, had been a basic formula to build on. Excellent public transport was apparently used by 75 per cent of the population. The separation of trash and products for re-cycling was also pursued with energy by three quarters of the population. Bicycle routes gave access to many kilometres of native forest and the city boasted that 98 per cent of the people who lived in Curitiba said they would never think of moving anywhere else.

Back in Rio I met someone who, at the time, could not dream of moving anywhere else. Throughout the Summit, visitors were offered information and guidance by a famous fugitive: the Great Train Robber, Ronnie Biggs. He was not going to appear in any of our Summit editions of *Outlook* (four altogether) but I was determined to go and meet him. He lived with his Brazilian born son (the key to keeping him safe from deportation) in a pleasant apartment near the city centre. He clearly missed London and his wife, who had settled in Melbourne, Australia.

He received regular visits from members of the old gang who had carried out the train robbery and had been released from prison after serving a fraction of that absurd thirty-year sentence. The best moment in a very genial meeting came when Ronnie took me out onto the terrace to show me a very colourful and attractive garden. I asked him if it was all his own work.

'Yes,' he said. 'I am quite a keen gardener. Always have been.' Laughing, he added, 'In fact, I think I should have taken up gardening rather than crime.'

6

Just Three of Us

There were just three of us in my generation of the Tidmarsh Family: My two cousins, Jill and her younger sister Lorna, and myself, the youngest of the three. We all grew up in the second half of the reign of King George V. I well remember the celebrations for his Silver Jubilee in 1935. All the pupils in my primary school were given a souvenir mug. King George was the first of our monarchs to be persuaded, in 1932, to make a Christmas broadcast on 'the wireless', to Britain and the furthest reaches of the Empire.

To be frank, none of the members of the Royal family could have made a career in broadcasting. All we remember of his successor, Edward VIII, was when he told us of his decision to abdicate because he could not do the job without the woman he loved at his side, the American divorcee, Wallis Simpson. George VI made a very courageous effort because of his speech impediment and became a much admired and inspirational figure throughout the Second World War, not least for staying in London with his family, the Queen and the two princesses, throughout the Blitz. Like millions of others we never failed to listen to his Christmas Day broadcasts.

King George V did make some visits to see his Empire, the most spectacular being in 1911 to India, where he was actually crowned as Emperor of India with Queen Mary as Empress. It was clearly a very wearing occasion and may have been responsible for making him decide that he would much prefer to stay at home building up his extraordinary stamp collection. When asked later in his reign if he was ready to make another trip, he apparently said quite vehemently that he was not.

'Abroad is awful,' he declared. 'I know, I have been there.'

George V died in 1935, four years before the start of the war that would see so many of his subjects sent abroad whether they liked it or not, fighting in Europe, the Middle East and the Far East, defending both Britain and his Empire.

For my two cousins the War in the forties was a very exciting time. They were both involved in 'clandestine activities' in China. Their father, one of my father's three younger brothers, was Capt. Percy James Tidmarsh. He had been appointed Adjutant at one of the many mansions all over Britain which had been taken over to train operatives working for SOE (Special Operations Executive). This particular one was at Beaulieu in the New Forest in Hampshire. The very important undercover role of the SOE can broadly be summed up as espionage, sabotage, and subversion in helping resistance groups. Two of its most famous members were women spies operating in occupied Europe: Violette Szabo, who was eventually caught and killed in the concentration camp at Ravensbrück, and Odette Churchill, who was also sent to Ravensbrück, but survived. My cousins in China, both eventually working in Kunming as the Japanese advanced, were certainly not used as spies and I am not exactly sure what subversive activities they may have been involved in.

When the war was over both Jill and Lorna married men who had been prisoners of the Japanese. Lance Walford, who married Jill, was a senior executive of the Shell Oil Company, based in Singapore. After being captured he was sent to work on the Thai-Burma Railway, constructing the infamous bridge over the River Kwai. The experience left him with a lasting loathing for the Japanese, as it did so many POWs who were fortunate to survive. Lorna's husband, Donald McAllister, was captured when Hong Kong fell. Later, after the war, his work took him frequently to Japan, so his experiences may not have left him quite so hostile.

I first met Lance when he was back with Shell and stationed in Singapore with Jill, when I was doing my National Service at RAF Seletar in 1948. Lorna also joined them there some time later, so all three of us have fond memories of 'Singers'. It was an experience which left me with an attachment to SE Asia and the Far East that has lasted all my life. I love a tropical climate. There is nothing like blue skies and sunshine for keeping me cheerful. In retirement I have often stopped off in Malaysia and Singapore on my way each year to spend two or three months in Australia to escape the British winter. Vietnam is also a favourite destination.

I just escaped being posted to Korea as a National Serviceman, but went there much later to make two editions of *Outlook*. Another favourite destination is The Philippines, though the difference between the very rich and the hopelessly poor in these islands is very depressing. I was once entertained by the British Consul in Cebu and told her that what the country really needed was not the current President, Fidel Ramos, but someone like Fidel Castro. She actually agreed.

Other places I have greatly enjoyed over the years include Borneo, Bali, Hong Kong, Bangkok and Japan. Not all of these adventures have been at the expense of the BBC. I made my first visit to Japan privately, enjoying the huge privilege of staying in a family home in Tokyo with basic *shóji* walls and rooms measured out in rectangular *tatami* mats. I have always admired the minimal approach to furnishing and decoration as practised by the Japanese. My bedroom actually had no bed. You had to lift up a flap close to the floor and there it all was concealed behind the wainscoting: extremely comfortable, full length futon mattress and a warm duvet. When you woke up in the morning you shut it all away again out of sight.

The morning also brought a rather enchanting little ritual. Next door was the room which had once belonged to the husband of my hostess, who had recently been widowed. It was still kept as his room; many of his clothes were still there. Every morning, between 7.00 and 8.00, there were footsteps in the corridor as the widow came to his room, slid open the door and rang a small bell to announce her arrival. She then started talking to him, presumably passing on the latest family gossip. When she had placed a cup of freshly made tea on the small altar that carried his picture, this charming ceremony was over and she left to get on with the day's chores. These included looking after one of those rather bleak Japanese gardens, made up almost entirely of stones. Not exactly the right environment for sitting out in a deck chair with a glass of wine, though such spots eliminate much of the need for back-breaking weeding.

I really enjoy Tokyo, especially the Underground, which is run with astonishing efficiency and time-keeping. There are moments in the rush hour when it could be absolute bedlam, requiring a strong force of packers all along the platform, to push passengers through the doors until the carriages are about to burst. At these moments it is as well to belong to one of the taller races so that you can actually see over the heads of the Japanese passengers. You can then be sure your travelling companion has not been swept out onto the platform at the last station and stranded.

My first visit to Tokyo got me addicted to Japanese food, especially *sashimi* (raw fish with a *Wasabi* dipping sauce). I could live on a Japanese diet, which is said to be very healthy, although I would have to take a break every so often for a deliciously spicy Indian curry or very slowly cooked lamb shanks.

The second time I was in Tokyo I was putting together another overseas edition of *Outlook*. We were on our way, in 1985, to the 40th anniversary of the bombing of Hiroshima. It provided a chance to experience the very best in high speed train travel: the Shinkansen. There is a moment on the journey from Tokyo to Hiroshima when you get a rather splendid view of Mount Fuji. But it is not a journey that gives you many chances to admire the Japanese countryside. The train keeps popping in and out of tunnels.

Hiroshima is now a spacious and modern city. Pictures of the devastation wreaked on August 6th 1945 show how little was left standing after the bomb, 'Little Boy', exploded at sixteen minutes past eight in the morning. One or two buildings, constructed with concrete to withstand earthquakes, didn't entirely collapse, such as the Czech designed Trade Centre on the banks of the river. The remains are still there, including the metal framework of the dome on the roof of the building. It is now the Hiroshima Peace Memorial and overlooks the site where the annual August 6th commemoration takes place.

My most vivid memory, however, is of the concrete step that once stood outside a bank. One end of it is blackened by the shadow of a human being going into the bank as the bomb burst overhead. Whoever it was, man or woman, was simply vaporised.

No air raid siren could have warned the population of Hiroshima what to expect. Indeed, none ever sounded as *Enola Gay*, and the two accompanying aircraft, were assumed to be on a photographic mission, so Japanese fighters were not sent up to engage them.

The target for the second bomb, 'Fat Man', three days later on August 9th, should have been Kokura. But when the B29 Superfortress arrived overhead the city was covered in cloud, and it was essential to be able to see both the target and the result, so the aircraft made for the secondary target, Nagasaki.

They arrived to find the weather there was much clearer. The cloud cover had broken. So the second – and so far the last – devastating nuclear weapon was launched. One of my neighbours in Brighton was actually there on that day. He had been taken prisoner while serving at RAF Seletar in Singapore, eventually being moved to a POW Camp on the outskirts of Nagasaki. Still going strong in his mid-eighties, he suffered none of the after-effects of radiation that killed so many Japanese in addition to those who died in the two explosions.

There are those who maintain that both Hiroshima and Nagasaki were war crimes. I do not take that view.

7

Our Listeners

The regular audience for all the programmes going out around the world from Bush House was somewhere in the region of 250–300 million. *Outlook* certainly had a healthy share of that. But we never really knew how many listeners we had in Britain. The transmitters were trained to focus on distant parts and leapt over the UK. But there is no doubt the British audience grew substantially in the middle of the night when Radio 4 went off the air and World Service took over that domestic frequency until six o'clock in the morning. *Outlook's* third edition thus became available shortly after 01.00 GMT. I have met quite a few listeners in Britain, among them Princess Margaret, who were World Service enthusiasts. She enjoyed visiting Bush House, staying to dinner with the management (best single malt Scotch Whisky provided) taking a midnight tour that often ended in the Continuity Studio.

On her way round one evening she popped into Studio C23 to chat to me after I had just come off the air with our second 'live' edition of *Outlook*. You could always tell, following one of these visits, that the Princess had stayed on well after midnight enjoying her tour – next morning the senior management all looked a bit fractured!

Frankie Howerd told us he too was a regular listener. He lived in Somerset. In that part of the country he could probably have heard the programme before Radio Four came off the air, as the World Service transmitters would be pointing out over the Atlantic to North and South America and the Caribbean.

Alan Whicker, who lived in the Channel Islands, was another regular. He came to the studio as a 'live' guest to talk about his own life, travelling all over the world for various BBC television programmes.

During the Second World War he was an officer with an army photographic unit, which is no doubt where he first learnt the skills that made him such an outstanding broadcaster. He gave me a copy of his autobiography *Within Whicker's World*, in which he wrote: 'John, thank you for making insomnia a pleasure!' Like my cousin Jill, living at the time in Suffolk, he was someone else who tuned in regularly in the middle of the night because he could not sleep.

At the end of the eighties I was able to meet, in their own countries, many listeners who had been obliged to tune in rather more furtively – and not just to the World Service in English but to several of the language services as well. As the wall dividing East and West crumbled, we set out to make editions of *Outlook* on the spot in Eastern Europe.

We started in Berlin. I had been there more than once in previous years, finding the atmosphere, the perceptible tension, rather exciting. It was certainly the only city where, travelling on the U-Bahn (the Underground) from West to East, you needed to carry your passport. Setting off from the West the train would pass through stations in the no-go zone that had long been closed and left completely deserted – Potsdamer Platz for example. Arriving at Friedrichstrasse station in the East you joined a queue, exactly like passing through Customs and Immigration at an airport. You also had to buy a small amount of East German marks. East Berlin certainly tried hard to present itself as the standard of life for the rest of East Germany. It was not, of course

I was, however, extremely delighted to find a bar close to Alexanderplatz station that sold my favourite tipple, draught Guinness. The Irish had been given special privileges in return for allowing the Soviet airline, Aeroflot, to land at Shannon on its way back and forth over the North Atlantic. Aeroflot was not welcome elsewhere in Western Europe.

I was in West Berlin for one of the best New Year's Eve parties I have ever known. It was 1989 and we were in front of the Brandenburg Gate. The Wall was now coming down, the process having begun a month earlier, and several of the revellers on the eastern side were helping to knock bits out of it. There were no longer any barriers at Brandenburg on that magical night. The *Volkspolizei* (VOPOs), the People's Police, had long since given up trying to stop East Berliners pouring through to the West. I don't think they ever really tried; there was plenty of unrestrained traffic going the other way. Some party-goers were sitting on top of the Wall, but I particularly remember a large group actually on the Brandenburg Gate, waving not only the German flag, with the hammer and sickle cut out of the middle but also the blue and white European flag. I tried to describe the scene for our first programme, speaking into a microphone which bore the initials BBC. We should have known better! I was frequently interrupted by revellers who clearly wanted to make me feel welcome; the Sekt (German champagne) was flowing freely and I lost count of the number of times I was offered a drink – from the bottle, naturally.

The morning after the night before the East Germans already had a clear view of their future – the European flags being waved on the top of the Brandenburg Gate had made that plain enough – a United Germany within the EU.

Inside East Germany, however, there were those who must have felt the need to get away rather urgently – the Communist collaborators. I remember visiting a modest suburban house which was already being ransacked. It had been the local headquarters of the Stasi, the Communist Secret Police. Had they managed, before leaving to shred all the evidence that might incriminate this neighbour or that as an odious informer?

It would be another five years before Russia managed to withdraw all its forces in East Gennany, at one time amounting to some four hundred thousand. I was actually at the suburban railway station from which the final military train pulled out on its way to St Petersburg. There were rather tearful scenes as some East Germans came to bid a fond farewell to those who had become close friends. I also gathered a few of the troops were less than happy to be going home, where the life style would not be as good as it had been for them in Germany.

Having survived that New Year's Eve in Berlin, we next had to make our way to Poland. Leaving the hotel, we asked our taxi driver to take us to the Ostbahnhof.

'I can't do that,' he said. 'I can just take you as far as one of the Check Points and there you must get another taxi on the other side.'

We assured him it was now possible to go all the way, and he agreed to give it a try. We arrived at the Ostbahnhof without any problems. Our driver was almost ecstatic.

'It is wonderful to be able to do that again,' he exclaimed.

So it was all aboard the night train to Warsaw in a very comfortable, First Class single sleeping compartment. Unlike the East Germans, the Poles did not at this stage have such a clear view of what the future held for them, although no-one had done more than they to bring down the Soviet hold on Eastern Europe by rejecting Communist rule.

It had all started with 'Solidarity', the introduction in the early eighties of an anti-Communist Trade Union and social movement in the Gdansk shipyards. Its leader, who would ultimately become President of Poland, was Lech Wałesa. At the beginning of the nineties I suspect very few Poles foresaw they would soon be in the European Union, and have the opportunity to live and work abroad, not least in Britain.

As far as I am concerned, they are all very welcome. I was reminded of why we should all have warm feelings towards the Poles when, in November 2007, I read an obituary in *The Times*. It was for Squadron Leader Tadeusz Andersz, one of the many Polish fighter pilots who came to help the RAF win the Battle of Britain. Altogether, some fifteen Polish fighter and bomber squadrons were based in Britain during the war. The gallant Squadron Leader had died at the age of eighty-nine.

Warsaw was virtually destroyed in the Second World War. The Nazis did that as they retreated before the advancing Red Army. There has been considerable rebuilding work, with some great effort made to restore the historic centre. They tell you that the best view in the city is from the top of the Cultural Centre, a truly hideous building representing the most appalling features of Soviet architecture. It was a gift from Joseph Stalin. It offers the best view of Warsaw because it is the only spot from which you cannot actually see it.

I have to say that the big moment for me on this tour of Eastern Europe came when we were in Prague in what was then still Czechoslovakia. I was in Wenceslas Square with a delightful lady called Mrs Dachnikova. We were talking about the 'Velvet Revolution' that brought down the Communist régime without bloodshed. Every night the Square would start to fill up, almost imperceptibly at first, with people leaving work. Before long it was absolutely packed as they quietly looked up at the statue of King Wenceslas and the parliament building behind, where the Communist government's days were now numbered.

Mrs Dachnikova told me that she lived with her daughter and son-in-law and her young grand-daughter in a fairly small flat. In the first few days of the Velvet Revolution she stayed home looking after the little girl. Then she told her daughter and son-in-law it was her turn to be there. She wanted to be a part of it. By the time she had finished her story we were at the bottom of the square and I thanked her and turned off my recorder. She then asked me if she could say something else, so I switched on again.

'I just wanted to thank the BBC,' she said, 'for all you did for us over the past forty years. We could not believe anything we heard on our own radio or the television or read in our newspapers. You told us what was really going on in the world. You gave us hope that one day things would change.'

Could the BBC World Service have a more beautiful testimonial? Thank you, Mrs Dachnikova. You will always be one of my favourite listeners.

There was one other moment during our tour of Eastern Europe that also lives with me quite vividly. We were in Hungary. One grey, gloomy and rather damp evening I was taken into the municipal cemetery, on the outskirts of Budapest. There, at the furthest point from the main gates, I was shown a number of unmarked burial mounds.

'Underneath that one,' said my guide, pointing to the large mound right in front of me, 'is Imre Nagy.'

He was the leader who paid dearly for the very brief Hungarian Revolution of October 1956, the event that was so rapidly to promote me from being a regional BBC reporter to a correspondent at the United Nations in New York. When the Soviet Union and other Warsaw Pact countries moved in to suppress the rebellion, Nagy and two of his associates were secretly put on trial and executed. Not long after my visit to the cemetery Imre Nagy was re-buried with full honours.

Towards the end of 1991, as we approached thirty years on the air, *Outlook* suddenly became rather famous, even in Britain. The Beirut hostages were starting to be released. First out, in August of that year, was the journalist John McCarthy. We had sent messages to him on his birthday, hoping he might hear them – and he did. At first the hostages had World Service passed through the wall to them from the prisoners who had a radio in an adjoining room. Eventually, they got their own Radio – the small portable that Terry Waite was allowed to keep when he arrived – and he knew exactly what frequency it should be tuned to, as he had long been a World Service fan.

Soon after his return home John McCarthy came to see us in Bush House and we offered him a job. For a long time I had been presenting *Outlook* three days a week. I was now keen to have more time off, so John took over the Wednesday edition. I found him to be most enjoyable company; he seemed comparatively unscathed by his dreadful experience.

The second release from Beirut came in November 1991: Terry Waite and the former Professor at the American University in Beirut, Thomas Sutherland. It was Sutherland who gave a fulsome tribute to World Service in general and *Outlook* in particular, mentioning both me and Barbara Myers by name. Barbara had for some time been presenting the programme on Monday and Tuesday. Calls at once started coming into Bush House from the media all over America wanting to know who we were. I just had time to make some sort of modest comment before setting off on a flight to Los Angeles and Honolulu, leaving Barbara to stand alone in the spotlight, which I have no doubt she greatly enjoyed. I was very happy to avoid all that, and instead, to be on my way to make programmes recalling the 'Day of Infamy': The 50th anniversary of the Japanese attack on Pearl Harbor.

Thanks to a very helpful American private pilot, who owned one of those delightful old Harvard trainers, I was able to fly the very route the Japanese took as they came over the north shore of the island of Maui in two waves, having taken off from aircraft carriers some 270 miles away.

I just got close enough to have a very clear view of the whole harbour before we made a tactful turn to starboard to return to the small airfield in the north of the island. But I had seen the target just as those Japanese airman had seen it fifty years earlier. The first wave attacked the American airfields, destroying more than 280 aircraft. The second wave was after the battleships, eventually damaging or destroying no fewer than eight of them, including the *Arizona*, which sank at its berth trapping 1,300 members of the crew inside. Their bodies are still there and the *Arizona* has become an extremely moving memorial. To pay your respects you stand on a platform from which you can see the hull of the ship just below. I noticed that quite a few Japanese visitors go there, some leaving messages of apology and regret as well as many of those delightful little folded paper cranes, another gesture of sorrow.

When I was there that December I discovered that Honolulu was a popular destination for Japanese tourists, particularly if they were getting married. Apparently it is much cheaper for the bride and groom to pay to fly out all the family and a few close friends and have, not only the wedding ceremony, but also the wedding breakfast in Honolulu rather than Japan.

Investigating the city of Honolulu ('It's a bit like a suburb of Los Angeles,' one local said to me) I was taken to the top of a hill which offered a perfect view of all the activity in the harbour below. It was a spot from which a Japanese agent, possibly someone posing as a tourist, was able to keep Tokyo fully informed of all the comings and goings. On the day, of the attack, however, one absolutely essential piece of information was missing. Admiral Yamamoto, who led the whole operation, had one question: 'What about the aircraft carriers?' To his great dismay he was told they were not there. They had gone out on exercise some hours before. It was those same aircraft carriers that would play a decisive role in inflicting substantial losses on Japan's Pacific Fleet some five months later at the Battle of Midway.

In the middle of the nineties I quietly and privately decided that I would sign no more contracts. My seventieth birthday was fast approaching and I already wanted to be able to avoid the British winter by spending those two or three months in Australia every year. I had recently bought a new house in Melbourne, where my son was now well established as the head of a department dealing with young sex offenders and restoring them to civilised society. I could happily have emigrated to Australia for good, but the other half of the family, my daughter Emma and her daughter Siân and my wife Pat, who runs what we call 'Family Headquarters' in Torquay, were likely to remain in Britain, at least for the time being. I also had ambitions to live in France. Emma has been working very successfully in Local Government, helping solve security problems for both business and residents.

8

The Great Betrayal

So it really was time to go. But what timing! Out of the blue the World Service was struck a blow that could well have destroyed it.

The Director General of the BBC, John Birt, and his ally Sir Christopher Bland, the BBC Chairman, proposed absorbing World Service within domestic radio and television. Bland was an old friend of Birt's from their days together in commercial television and Birt had been instrumental in getting him the post of BBC Chairman.

At first I thought the idea must have originated with the bunch of charlatans called 'management consultants' whom Birt had been employing, at vast expense, to guide him through the process of 'restructuring' the BBC. I later learned that 'The Gang of Two', as I called them, were themselves solely responsible for it.

Sam Younger, who was the World Service Managing Director at the time of this fiasco, and deeply opposed to it, was told by one of those 'consultants' that they had absolutely nothing to do with it. Nor for that matter had the Foreign Office, which finances the whole of World Service. Indeed, the day before Birt and Bland were to make their plans public, one of the conspirators raised a somewhat embarrassing question.

'Have we told the Foreign Office? Will they be joining us?'

The answer was 'No.' I am not entirely sure what response was received when they decided to put in a rather late phone call to invite someone from the FO to be present. I don't imagine it was very cordial. The Foreign Secretary himself, Malcolm Rifkind may well have been distracted by what eventually proved to be an unsuccessful attempt to save his parliamentary seat in Scotland. When the conspirators were called into the Foreign Office some time later to see him, however, an eye witness told me that Bland, in particular, was given such a scathing dressing down they had never seen him so shaken.

The idea of diminishing and severely damaging World Service created instant uproar, not only around the world, but notably in Britain. Three of the most recent Managing Directors – three of the best – Gerald Mansell, Austin Kark and John Tusa, immediately launched a 'Save World Service' campaign. Among the first to join was Lord Healey, a former Foreign Secretary, who promised to lead the battle in the House of Lords.

'The World Service,' he said, 'has never been more important in getting across Britain's message.'

Another irate protest came from a former member of the Board of Governors, Baroness James, the author P.D. James.

She said: 'I don't know whether to be more appalled by the decision itself or the way it has been arrived at. Arrogance, extraordinary arrogance! I would like to say to both John Birt and the Chairman, "They do not own the BBC."'

I learned some time later that two existing members of the Board of Governors decided to resign, feeling they had failed in their duty. They admitted as much to Sam Younger, who stayed on briefly as Managing Director through all the initial turmoil.

There were those who thought Sam should have resigned instantly. I don't agree. By staying on he was eventually able to insist that World Service must retain a separate newsroom closely linked to all the Language Services. For that we must also give a small amount of credit to Bland who supported his view.

I was looking recently through a list of some of the international figures who joined the 'Save World Service' campaign. Mikhail Gorbachev was one of them. Archbishop Desmond Tutu of Capetown another. There was also an e-mail from a man revered by millions. It read: 'I am appealing to the British Government, the BBC's Board of Governors and its senior management to save the BBC's distinct and independent entity. The only people pleased to see the BBC World Service damaged or destroyed will be the dictators and authoritarian régimes whose policies deprive their citizens – for whom the BBC is a lifeline – of freedom and information.' It came from the Dalai Lama.

The effect of all this uproar on *Outlook* was not immediately apparent. The programme remained based on the eighth floor of Bush House, but was now apparently linked to a group of Radio Four programmes, which included the excellent *Woman's Hour.* The head of this department was Anne Winder, someone I had known as a junior producer in the seventies when I presented the seven o'clock evening news programme on Radio Four called *Newsdesk.* I feared the worst.

I assume it was Miss Winder who sent a representative from Broadcasting House to tell her what *Outlook* was all about and, more sinisterly, to make suggestions for the future. I cannot now recall the name of this person, but the *Outlook* staff soon started referring to her as 'Miss Disastrous', a play on her real name.

I was completely unaware of what was going on in the background, I turned up every Thursday and Friday at 10.00 a.m. to present the programme and made my way home again just after four o'clock in the afternoon. I did once ask a producer to put up an idea at one of *Outlook's* planning meetings. You will not be surprised to know that it involved a replica of the *Matthew* making its way across the Atlantic to Newfoundland to commemorate that famous journey made 500 years ago from Bristol. I thought we could get the RAF to fly us out over the Atlantic to talk to the *Matthew* below us and then go on to record its arrival in Canada. The whole idea was instantly dismissed by Miss Disastrous who said it was 'too British'. Someone from another World Service department took over the idea and made an excellent programme.

Eventually, I had a private meeting with Miss Disastrous who told me that they (presumably she and Winder) felt that *Outlook* needed 'refreshing'. This is often code for: 'We don't really know what to do, so let us start by changing the presenters.' I was still keeping very quiet about my intention to leave and they may have had some difficulty in deciding how they could treat me, bearing in mind that I had recently been awarded an OBE in recognition of my services to broadcasting.

The deal they offered me was to give up presenting the programme twice a week, but to take over a whole programme once a month with a major interview. I solved their problem by saying it was an idea that would suit me perfectly, as long as I could put two or three recorded editions in the bank before taking my winter break in Australia. As for poor Barbara Myers, she was simply told to go. Shameful! She was replaced by a presenter from domestic radio, Heather Peyton, and my job was given to a delightful fellow called Fred Dove who, despite being disabled as a result of his mother taking thalidomide while she was pregnant, coped wonderfully. He was actually Captain of the England Disabled cricket team.

I enjoyed doing those twelve interviews that year, even though it meant staying on with the World Service longer than I intended. Finally, however, I made it clear that enough was enough. Very generously, they signalled my final departure with a whole edition looking back over my 44 years with the BBC, particularly the 34 or so with World Service. I was interviewed by Fred – though I supplied the questions!

I don't really know what has happened to *Outlook* since I left. I have hardly ever heard of it. I gather there were quite a few listeners wanting to know what had happened to me. One e-mail from America was clearly rather critical of one edition of the programme. It read: 'John Tidmarsh, where are you when we need you?'

My final sortie overseas for *Outlook* came when I was asked if I would put together an edition from Somalia, certainly one of the more dangerous places I have been. I was told I could decline if I felt I didn't want to go, so it was not part of a cunning plan to get rid of me! I If I had had any reason for turning it down it would only have been that that part of Africa was a region about which I knew very little. I only knew that Somalia had virtually fallen apart in the early nineties, tribal warfare bringing violence, misery and famine to the whole country; it was a desperately sad place.

We set off first to Nairobi in Kenya. There we made arrangements to join the American crew of a Hercules transport, carrying food and other essential supplies for the Red Cross. We left Nairobi some time before dawn, planning to arrive at our first stop, Mogadishu, the capital of Somalia, shortly after sunrise. The hope was that we would arrive at a slightly quieter time of day in a city where law and order had broken down almost completely.

Once we had the airport at Mogadishu in sight the captain wanted to know if it was safe to land. Someone on the ground radioed back to say it looked fairly quiet. Nevertheless, the captain thought he ought to take a closer look for himself, so we flew the length of the runway at no more than 100 feet before turning steeply out into the ocean on the starboard side, coming back in again at the top end of the runway to make a safe landing.

The next problem was getting some of the cargo, meant for Mogadishu, unloaded before any of the local gunmen turned up to get their hands on it. Within less than half an hour we were on our way again to our final destination, much further north, at a place called Belet Huen. Here a small crowd was waiting to greet us in front of the ramshackle tin hut that served as the airport terminal. It bore a roughly made sign with the inscription: 'Welcome to Belet Huen International Airport'!

We were to stay with the Red Cross, within their well-guarded compound. Almost immediately I heard in the distance a short burst of machine-gun fire. A sudden outbreak of fighting in the town centre? A brief gesture of jubilation? Or just some members of a warlord's army reminding the local population that they were in charge? Later that day I decided to take a look at the centre of town. There I watched an open truck come through the market with four heavily armed men sitting in the back, brandishing their Kalashnikovs – the local 'peacekeepers'.

I have one indelible memory of Belet Huen, a photographic image permanently stored in the brain. The day after our arrival the wonderful Red Cross took us to the large refugee centre they were running. Every day more desperate and dishevelled people arrived, often whole families, many of them having travelled great distances to find sanctuary. How many died *en route* from lack of water and food, or sheer fatigue? Who knows? Even among those who finally made it all hope may have been lost. I remember one particular family – father and son, mother and small daughter. The mother and the little girl were lying inside a shelter made of sticks and small branches, shaped rather like an igloo. I took a very quick look, anxious not to be too intrusive at such a desperate moment. The woman lay there, glassy-eyed and unseeing, clearly close to death. There was absolutely nothing the

Red Cross could do to save her. By the end of the day both the mother and her little daughter were dead. It is an image I can never forget. The father and son survived.

9

'With Me in the Studio Today...'

There were days when turning up for another 'live' edition of *Outlook* in Bush House could seem more challenging than usual. For example, when they told me that my 'live' studio guest the following day would be A.J. Ayer (Freddie Ayer), universally acknowledged as the leading expert on the philosopher Wittgenstein. Time to go home and do a little swotting up on 'logical positivism'. As we went on the air I could see some of my colleagues looking rather gleefully through the studio window, wondering how I would cope. 'Freddie' was very good company. Before we went on the air we chatted a bit about football. He was a great soccer fan supporting the North London club Tottenham Hotspur. As for the interview, we talked a little about his days in Vienna – after graduating in philosophy at Christ Church, Oxford, he went to Austria to investigate logical positivism. Then, at the age of 24, he wrote a book about it, which brought him public recognition. It was called *Language, Truth and Logic*.

It was while we were talking about Wittgenstein that I enjoyed one of my favourite moments in *Outlook*. Listening very, very carefully to what Freddie was saying, I rather rashly decided to make sure that I (and the listeners) had understood.

'In other words,' I said, 'so and so and so and so and so.'

I have forgotten the actual words ... but I have never forgotten Freddie's reply.

'Exactly,' he said.

Glancing through the window to those on the production side of the studio, I caught sight briefly of dear John Thompson, our resident newspaper reviewer, grinning broadly and nodding in approval.

Another 'live' studio guest who, on the face of it, might have appeared a bit of a challenge, was someone who had been on stage in theatres all over the world and never uttered a single word: the great French mime artist, Marcel Marceau. He, too, proved to be most enjoyable company. He talked first about growing up in the lovely city of Strasbourg. He was just fourteen when the Second World War broke out and the family moved to Limoges, in what would become Vichy France during the German occupation. At first he thought he would like to be a painter but, just after the war ended, he became very interested in mime, which requires, he said, a certain amount of athleticism, like being a dancer. We talked briefly about its origins – Commedia dell'Arte, clowns and pantomime – and the use made of it by people like Chaplin and Keaton in early silent films. But Marceau claims to have been the first to take it to America in 1955 as what he called 'dramatic theatre without words', the emphasis being on theatre. He had recently been touring China where he was a great success, finding his audience laughed at the same things as the Europeans, the British and the French. Mime was a tradition that only declined after the First World War. One of his scenes from everyday life, as he called them, was the man trying to find his way out of a glass tank – both sad and hilarious. Marcel Marceau was in his eighties when he died in the autumn of 2007.

Mime may not have been suitable for Radio, but ventriloquists were able to get away with their art. Edgar Bergan in America and Peter Brough with 'Archie Andrews' in Britain. It was in the popular show *Educating Archie* that I first remember hearing Monica, the cheeky schoolgirl, the character which was the first big break for the person who was without doubt one of our favourite guests: the comedienne who later became a much acclaimed actress, Beryl Reid. She was only four when she told her parents that she wanted to go on the stage. Her father was horrified.

'He said he would rather see me dead at his feet.'

Her mother was more sympathetic and arranged for her to have dancing lessons.

'I realised that up there on a stage is where you could show off a bit.'

When she was some years older she won a talent contest in Manchester which gave her the chance to appear in London for a week at the Astoria cinemas in Brixton and the Old Kent Road where, in those days, there was often a brief interlude of 'live' entertainment between the films.

But it was the play about a long-running soap opera that turned her into a really big star: *The Killing of Sister George*. When she was offered the chance to play the lesbian Sister George, she told me she took advice from 'two chaps who were in my life at the time'. One told her not to touch it with a barge pole.

'It will ruin your image,' he said.

The other thought it was worth taking a chance. So she did. With Eileen Atkins (later Dame Eileen) the production went first on one of those pre-West End tours.

The reception in the provinces was awful. In Hull, she told me, it was so cold and disapproving that local shops almost refused to sell anything to members of the cast. Back in London, however, it was a triumph and Beryl went on to make the film version with Susannah York. After Sister George she next appeared on the London stage in Joe Orton's *Entertaining Mr Sloane*.

'So from a Lesbian I suddenly became an ageing nymphomaniac,' she said, laughing.

Beryl told me how she then moved on to appear in Restoration comedy: first *The School for Scandal* and then as Mrs Malaprop in *The Rivals*. The part was a particular challenge for her as she was dyslexic.

When we finally got to talking about Honey Pot Cottage, her home on the banks of the River Thames near Windsor, Beryl was able to give the whole world some excellent advice on getting rid of visitors who call at an unwelcome moment. She had just got home after a difficult day with a particularly annoying director. Wanting to relax quietly, to wind down, she had 'slipped into my pink cat suit' and poured a large glass of something when the phone rang. It was her neighbour to warn her that two people had landed from the river at the bottom of the garden and were approaching the house. She went out to meet them and said how delighted she was to see them, but sorry she could not invite them in as 'I am in bed with someone I've only just met'. Showing great understanding, they left!

The incident occurred when she was living on her own with eight cats, one called Dimly. However, she did have what she called 'gentlemen callers'. There was an occasion when she was a bit tired, and probably rather tiddly after a summer lunch with some friends; after they had all gone home she felt rather hot and steamy, so she took off all her clothes, lay down naked on her bed and went to sleep.

'When I woke up,' she said, 'I found a note pushed through the letter box which read: "Your windows have been cleaned."'

10

'Interesting People'

'You must meet lots of very interesting people.' I wonder how many times someone has said that to me. In *Outlook* alone over the years I must have enjoyed the opportunity to talk to between two and three hundred people, mainly as 'live' guests in the studio. Fortunately, I kept my own recordings of some I particularly remember, like the three I have just written about. Let me include a few more.

Katharine Graham

Katharine Graham was once called 'the owner of the newspaper that forced a President out of office'. When I interviewed her she dismissed that idea as an exaggeration.

'There were others who played their part,' she said.

Yet there is no question that the *Washington Post*, with reporters Bob Woodward and Carl Bernstein, and the editor Ben Bradlee, was hugely instrumental in bringing down Richard Nixon in August 1974.

Unfortunately, I never met Katharine Graham face to face. When we talked we were three thousand miles apart. She was in our studio in Washington and I was in Bush House in London. Yet together we created a whole edition of *Outlook* as we talked about her newly published, 600-page autobiography titled *Personal History*.

The *Washington Post* was actually bought by her father, Eugene Meyer, at a bankruptcy auction in 1930. He paid $825,000 dollars for it and, in the early stages, it lost a million dollars a year. However, the Meyer family was extremely rich and, though she told me her parents were very strict, she enjoyed a privileged childhood. They had two houses in Washington and a ranch in Wyoming; they also spent time relaxing on various yachts. She married in 1940 a man she thought 'terribly attractive, gifted and brilliant' whom she adored. His name was Philip Graham.

He first became publisher of the *Washington Post* and then later Chairman, when her father died in 1959. Unfortunately, Philip Graham suffered from a mental disorder, which brought on several breakdowns and he was eventually admitted to a psychiatric hospital in Washington DC. On a week-end release from there he joined her in their home and committed suicide. That is when she took over, first as publisher and later as Chairman of the Board. She was described by some as 'the most powerful woman in America'. It was certainly unusual in those days for a woman to have such a prominent job, although she had also established by then a reputation as one of the leaders of Washington society.

Katharine was the one who brought Ben Bradlee to be Editor of the *Post*, someone she would lean on heavily throughout the period of often vicious threats against the paper from the Nixon administration as the work of Bob Woodward and Carl Bernstein slowly and carefully unfolded.

'I would go to Bradlee almost daily to ask for re-assurance. How do we know we are right? How do we know we are not being misled?'

Bradlee told her that they were getting back-up, not just from the Democrats, but also from Republican sources. On top of that they had never been misled by the special source that Woodward had developed.

'We called him "Deep Throat",' she said. 'He was named after a dirty movie that had just been released.'

I asked her if she knew who Deep Throat was.

'No,' she replied. 'I once asked Bob who it was and he looked so stricken I just said, "Oh, don't worry. It's all right."'

She never did know the name. She died a few years before W. Mark Felt, a former Deputy Director of the FBI, admitted in June 2005 that he was the man, Deep Throat, who advised Woodward to 'follow the money'.

I have huge admiration for Woodward, Bernstein and Bradlee, and I am sure many journalists of my generation feel the same. They kept the secret until Felt himself came out into the open.

I managed to insert near the end of the interview a recording of something Woodward himself said: 'Unfortunately, standards in journalism have changed. The weird, the coarse, the stupid, the sensational gossip, have been increasingly influential. The standards of Katharine Graham, Ben Bradlee, Carl Bernstein and me hold less force in the profession of journalism today.'

Women Prime Ministers

I managed to get a brief interview with Benazir Bhutto, not when she was Prime Minister of Pakistan, but on the day she announced she had just agreed to an arranged marriage. 'What,' I asked rather mischievously, 'is a former President of the Oxford Union doing embarking on an "arranged" marriage?'

'Well,' she said, 'quite often they work better and last rather longer.'

In her case it certainly turned out to be true. Her husband was still at her side when she was so tragically assassinated in 2007 while campaigning to be once again Pakistan's Prime Minister.

I met and interviewed Margaret Thatcher for a whole *Outlook* programme some years after she had left No. 10 and had just published her autobiography, *The Downing Street Years*. We met at what was then her London office. I began by suggesting it was a very long way from Grantham and the family grocer's shop, where she grew up, to No 10. Downing Street.

She told me she had never thought of a career in politics when she was young; her degree was in Chemistry.

'But the grocer's shop was the place where I learnt so much about people,' she said. 'It was a private shop and a place where they had time to stop and talk.'

She couldn't even think about trying to get into Parliament until MPs were much better paid. She added that it was still very much a man's world with a man's club atmosphere.

Early on she had said she thought there would never be a woman Prime Minister in her lifetime. When the moment came, did the Tories choose her because they were in some trouble and thought a woman PM would be an election winner? She dismissed that idea.

'They chose me because they knew what I believed and thought a fresh approach was needed.'

She denied the story that, at her first Cabinet meeting, she made it perfectly clear she was now in charge.

'I did not believe in a Prime Minister just acting as a chairman, going round the Cabinet table asking "What do you think?" So I led from the front. Perhaps they didn't always like it.'

Not quite the same woman who enjoyed listening to all those customers in the grocer's shop!

She admitted that there had been a lot of disagreement with Cabinet ministers from time to time, but denied there had been any violent scenes.

'They were just active and dynamic,' she said.

Yet, after eleven and half years in office, it was the members of her own Cabinet who finally ousted her. They rebelled against what they saw as her dictatorial style and accused her of being irrational and erratic.

She maintained there were two sorts of people in politics: 'The faint hearts and the brave hearts. After going through a tough time some wanted to take it easy and consolidate. But you can't just sit back,' she said. 'Sitting back was not for me.'

When it became clear she no longer enjoyed enough support to win a second vote to confirm her leadership of the Party – her colleagues 'hadn't got the guts to fight' – she went to that final Cabinet meeting to announce her resignation. It was a tearful affair, many of those present apparently looking fixedly down at the top of the table. She refused to name for me on the air those she felt had let her down. 'You'll have to read the book.'

How did she see her legacy, apart from victories in the Falklands and over the Trades Unions?

'Was there ever enough room in Thatcherism to look after the less fortunate, the unemployed, the poor, the homeless?' I asked.

'The only way you could create wealth and manage to do all of that was through a Thatcherite-Adam Smith enterprise economy,' she declared.

Did she still feel bitter about her final demise?

'I don't feel bitter at all,' she said. 'By the time you have done the tough things I had to do you make a lot of enemies. I was never defeated by the people. I kept the confidence of the British people and the Nation. The reputation of Britain rode high throughout when I left, and that was my great satisfaction.'

So now you know!

The Prime Minister whose company I most enjoyed was in office for only five months. Kim Campbell was elected by the ruling Conservative Party in Canada to take over from Brian Mulroney, when he retired in 1993. She narrowly ousted the other candidate for the job, Jean Charest. She took over in June, but an election was due five months later in October. At the time the Conservatives, who had been in power for nine years, were deeply unpopular, not least for introducing a General Sales Tax. The Canadian voters let them know it – the election left the party with just two seats, neither of which was Kim Campbell's. Did the Conservatives think that appointing her as Canada's first woman Prime Minister might just be enough to save their necks? She more or less dismissed that idea, saying that gender was not a very significant factor in Canadian politics. She had, after all, been the country's first woman Attorney General.

We met in Los Angeles where she had become Canada's Consul General and seemed remarkably happy. It was her fiftieth birthday.

'I am just getting on now with the second half of my life,' she said.

I asked if politics would still play any part in it.

'I have resigned myself,' she replied, 'to being just a middle-aged states-person rather than getting back into the electoral fray.'

She was writing a book and practising very hard on her new 'cello in the hope of joining some friends to give a concert in her native Vancouver.

'Initially,' she continued, 'some people seemed disappointed I didn't have a nervous breakdown. The election was devastating. I wanted to be Prime Minister because I thought I knew what the country needed. I wanted to lead. But if that is the worst thing that happens to me, I will have led a charmed life.'

Three of Kim Campbell's grandparents came from Scotland, members of what the Canadians jokingly call the 'MacMafia'.

'Canada was overwhelmingly settled by Scots,' she said.

Her mother's family, however, arrived originally from mainland Europe, coming ashore in Massachusetts in 1650.

She saw an important part of her present role to be raising the profile of Canada as a very distinct and different society, not just a blander version of the United States.

'Canadians themselves are among the worst navel gazers, yet so many of the leading talents here in Los Angeles, in Hollywood, are actually Canadians.'

I greatly enjoyed meeting Kim Campbell who, with her blonde hair and blue eyes, was a student at the LSE (the London School of Economics) opposite Bush House at the same time as Mick Jagger.

Henry Kissinger

Within days of winning the American Presidential Election in 1968, and weeks before his inauguration, Richard Nixon decided to get to grips with what he saw as the most urgent and difficult problem he would have to face: extricating America from Vietnam. He asked Henry Kissinger to come and see him. The meeting took place in private, just the two of them.

'He told me he wanted me to be his chief negotiator and asked me to make contact with North Vietnam at once, before he had even been sworn in as President.'

Formal peace talks would eventually take place in Paris at the invitation of President Pompidou, but behind the scenes Kissinger would be secretly meeting Le Duc Tho, the main representative of the North Vietnamese.

'The public talks,' he said, 'turned into a stale repetition of standard positions. So at first did our secret talks.'

Each morning when they met Le Duc Tho would give him little lectures on Marxist philosophy. Not so little on some occasions – he could drone on for forty-five minutes.

'It was tedious but I knew how to keep my patience. It was my job. Normally I am not very good at patience.'

Nevertheless, Kissinger told me, he found Le Duc Tho an impressive figure.

'He had done nothing in his life except fight foreigners. His purpose was to break our spirit by saying the same thing every day, word for word. Except one day he said, "You make a big effort and we will make an effort." I said, "Did I notice you dropped an adjective here?" He said, "I am so glad you noticed it."'

Kissinger explained that, basically, he was seeking to separate the military from the political, negotiating a military exit by America, providing the North Vietnamese gave re-assurance about a political process that would leave the future of Vietnam to the Vietnamese people.

I asked how many members of Nixon's administration knew about the secret talks. His reply was, 'The Secretary of State, the Secretary of Defence, the Ambassador in Saigon. They didn't mind. They were delighted to tie the can of Vietnam to my tail. There were no great volunteers for negotiations that were bound to end with little glory.'

Why did Nixon take it all on his own shoulders? Why didn't he go to Congress and say, 'This is what we need to do'?

Kissinger said, 'My recommendation was that he should go to Congress, but he thought it would be an abdication of executive responsibility.'

Did he end up with a great admiration for Nixon?

'He was an acquired taste for me,' he said. 'I had opposed him for twelve years, but he had a far sighted and capable view on Foreign Policy and great courage in carrying it out against violent opposition – the opening to China, détente with the Communist world.

I finally asked Kissinger how he thought history was going to see Nixon, a president who left office in disgrace.

Kissinger replied, 'I saw him the night before he resigned and told him that history would treat him more kindly than his contemporaries. Eventually, his funeral restored him to public acceptance.'

Sammy Cahn

From time to time we left our home in Studio C23 in Bush House, Centre Block, to find a studio that had a piano. An occasion I remember with enormous pleasure was when our 'live' studio guest for the day was the great lyricist, winner of four Academy Awards, Sammy Cahn. He was nominated for an Oscar no fewer than thirty times, collaborating with Jule Styne on songs for many films and musicals. In 1954 the first Oscar came – for the song 'Three Coins in the Fountain'.

The son of Jewish immigrants from Poland, he had four sisters and was born in New York on the Lower East Side.

'You couldn't get any lower on the East side than where I grew up,' he said.

In partnership with Jimmy Van Heusen he wrote dozens of songs for Frank Sinatra; he became known as Sinatra's personal lyricist – 'All the Way', 'High Hopes', 'Call me Irresponsible', 'Love and Marriage', 'Saturday Night is the Loneliest Night of the Week', 'The Tender Trap', 'I'll Walk Alone', 'My Kind of Town', to name just a few.

It was a song he wrote for the Jimmy Lunceford Orchestra, 'Rhythm is our Business', that opened the way for his meeting with Sinatra.

'It was that song,' he told me, 'that stamped me as a Band writer and I got a call from Tommy Dorsey, leader of one of the top big bands of the day and a trombone player. Tommy Dorsey was one of the really, really great talents. He could take a breath and blow for eighteen bars without having to take another.'

Frank Sinatra was Dorsey's vocalist and, according to Sammy, that is eventually where Sinatra's own style of singing came from, turning his voice away from the pitch of a violin into that of a viola.

I told Sammy Cahn that I had always had a vision of song writers like him, back in the twenties, thirties and forties, rushing into a music publisher's office excitedly waving a piece of paper, and saying, 'I've just written this.' His reply? 'You have seen too many B Movies!'

He did, however, have a lovely story of being with a music publisher in Los Angeles. It was a ferociously hot day and someone suggested they all go down to the beach.

'I said, "Why don't we stay here and write a winter song?"'

They did. It was called 'Let it snow, let it snow, let it snow.'

Sammy Cahn told me, 'There is no career quite as rewarding as successful song writing. You can be walking down the street and the fellow walking in front of you is humming one of your songs. Walk into a restaurant and the pianist is playing one of your songs. Walk into an elevator and you can hear another.'

He made this same comment when talking once to a group of students studying architecture. 'Can song writing really offer greater rewards than architecture?' asked one student.

Answer: 'Who walks down the street humming a building?'

Case closed.

Throughout the programme Sammy Cahn used our beautifully tuned grand piano to re-call various hits, including that famous Tommy Dorsey signature tune, 'Getting Sentimental Over You'. He told us he had also written a song about *Outlook*; we kept the audience in suspense until the end of the programme. To the tune of 'It's Magic' it went like this:

The hours and hours it took,
But now, at last I'm on *Outlook*,
It's magic.
And though he can be harsh
I love it here with John Tidmarsh,
It's magic.

The last verse was:

I can't believe that I'm
Getting so much *Outlook* time,
It's magic.
But I don't have to say
The payment that I'll take away
Is tragic.

We paid no fees to our studio guests, though we might sometimes send a car to collect them. Most were only too pleased to join us to promote a book, a film, a theatre performance, or maybe just themselves.

On one occasion, however, we were the ones who had to pay for our own transport. Our guest, in a memorable recorded edition of the whole programme, was providing the piano. The rendezvous was the Golders Green Hippodrome in North London.

Dudley Moore

The lovely Dudley was rehearsing for performances he was giving with the BBC Concert Orchestra – an eclectic mixture of Gershwin, Mozart and jazz, plus some amiable chat to the audience. We talked first about his childhood, which had not been very happy. Born in Dagenham in Essex he grew up as a rather small boy, handicapped by a club foot. It made him an easy target for bullies. Music became his refuge: first the violin, then both the piano and the organ. He told me that his great passion was Bach.

'I often get out of bed in the morning and pop down to the piano to play one of the Preludes,' he said.

'Is that a better start to the day than a breakfast of orange juice and cornflakes, eggs and bacon?' I asked.

'Yes,' he said 'it sets me up for the day. He was such a wonderful composer.'

The great watershed in his life was winning an organ scholarship to Magdalen College, Oxford. There he first met Alan Bennett and performed with him in cabaret. Through Alan Bennett he subsequently met Jonathan Miller and Peter Cook, the four of them devising the hugely successful satirical review *Beyond the Fringe*.

He didn't go into much detail (and I didn't press him) but merely said it was an American lady who made him decide to stay in Los Angeles, where he had been performing with Peter Cook in *Dud and Pete*. Who can forget those hilarious conversations that always seemed to bring Dud to the verge of imploding as he tried to stifle the urge to laugh?

'It was when I was having one of my regular sessions of psychotherapy that I found myself in the same group as Blake Edwards, who was about to direct a film called *10* starring Bo Derek. We became friendly and some time later he phoned me to say that George Segal had dropped out and the part in the film was mine. Bo Derek was terrific, a superstar and a sex symbol, but I had no idea *10* would be such a success.'

The film also turned Dudley into a superstar and a sex symbol, though modestly he was rather diffident about describing himself as such. It led to the film *Arthur* with John Gielgud earning an Oscar in his role as the manservant trying to cope with Arthur's follies. Dudley was undoubtedly one of our *Outlook* favourites. What a tragedy that he should die so young from a rare brain disease! He was only sixty-six.

Richard Attenborough

'Do you share your younger brother David's infectious enthusiasm for the world of nature and everything in it?'

'Well certainly not all those creepy crawly things. Absolutely not.'

Having got that out of the way I could now concentrate on the astonishing career of the actor on stage ... he was actually in the first production of *The Mousetrap* which, in 2008, was still running after 56 years – and in films (he had just played a leading role in *Jurassic Park*). Above all, I wanted to talk about his association with what I regard as two of the great films of the 20th century: *Oh What A Lovely War* and *Gandhi*, which was his triumph as a film director. It was another of those recorded interviews that ran for the whole of an *Outlook* programme.

He came from a family of academics and his initial stage experience was acting in school plays. At seventeen he won a scholarship to the Royal Academy of Dramatic Art in London.

'It was wartime so there were not many contestants, but I had to live on just two pounds, ten shillings a week.'

His earliest inspiration came from Charlie Chaplin, whom he first saw on film, then live in London.

'Seeing someone who could make you laugh and cry at the same time, I thought that was magic.'

He was only eighteen when he played Pinkie, the nasty, brutal little crook (whose character is the same age) in the film *Brighton Rock*, based on the novel by Grahame Greene. How important was that in launching his career in films?

'Very important. It was a phenomenal break.'

He told me that he has a great affection for Brighton and the part it has played in his career. He was back there again when he transformed for the screen the hugely successful stage musical *Oh! What a Lovely*

War, first produced by Joan Littlewood at the Theatre Royal, Stratford, in East London. It parodies the murderous and mindless military incompetence that cost so many millions of lives in Northern France and Flanders in the First World War. Attenborough chose to set the film on Brighton's West Pier as if it were one of those Seaside Follies, traditionally staged in the summer for visiting holidaymakers.

Some critics thought it did not do enough to recall the appalling casualties. Personally I thought the extremely moving closing scene said it all, as we watched the little crosses gradually cover the huge expanse of the Sussex Downs above Brighton – an unforgettable image.

I then moved on to what was undoubtedly his greatest film role as an actor: John Christie, the ghastly serial killer at 10, Rillington Place in London's Notting Hill. When his women victims were dead he had sex with them.

Gassing his victims from the domestic supply was his technique, on the pretext that, once they lost consciousness, he would be able to carry out the successful abortion which they had wanted.

'We did it in Rillington Place. I found it very disturbing playing the part of this frightening character,' he said. 'The house was pulled down the week after we finished filming. I did it because I am opposed to capital punishment.'

The rather simple, and entirely innocent, Timothy Evans was wrongly charged with the first of the murders and eventually hanged. It was a terrible miscarriage of justice that did a great deal to assist the later campaign for the abolition of capital punishment.

Gandhi was undoubtedly Richard Attenborough's greatest contribution to the history of cinema. Back in the sixties, he told me, he was completely bowled over by a book on Gandhi's life, given to him by a friend from the Indian High Commission in London, next door to Bush House.

'It took me twenty years to get around to the point when I thought I would like to direct a major film of Gandhi's life.'

It was certainly worth waiting for. It turned out to be a masterpiece.

I asked Richard if he still had any secret ambitions. How about becoming a song and dance man?

'Absolutely!' he said. 'That has always been a secret ambition. *Chorus*

Line was about the happiest film I ever made. Living in a Broadway Theatre for about seven weeks I was in my seventh heaven.'

Audrey Hepburn

Hundreds of famous faces came to talk to me in the *Outlook* studio. But sometimes, as I have said, in the case of Dudley Moore in the middle of rehearsals, we had to go to them to snatch a few moments while they were heavily engaged doing something else.

So it was with one of the most beautiful women I ever met: the enchanting Audrey Hepburn. She was in the middle of a national tour explaining her role as a goodwill ambassador for UNICEF. That is what we talked about, all too briefly. With more time to chat in the studio I would have liked to hear about her life in The Netherlands during the German occupation in the Second World War. She was there with her Dutch mother who had returned after separating from her British father.

Unlike Ann Frank, she was not forced to hide away for fear of being sent to a concentration camp, though she was certainly suffering from malnutrition when the war ended. That would have given her something in common with so many of the children she would later be meeting in the Third World.

I did not realise when I met her that her days were numbered. There was no sign of the stomach cancer that would shortly end her life. Her main anxiety, as we ended the brief interview, appeared to be quickly finding something to eat for lunch before her next appointment.

Anticipating some of our 'live' guests, I thought more than once that I could be facing a bit of a challenge – Morecombe and Wise, for example. In fact, they were great fun. There was a time when Christmas entertainment on television was unthinkable without *The Morecombe and Wise Show*. Then there was Spike Milligan, the Goon himself, scriptwriter of the much loved *Goon Show* with Harry Secombe and Peter Sellers.

He must have delighted a huge section of our audience when he spoke so warmly of his happy memories of growing up in India and Burma, where his father was in the British Indian Army. During the Second World War, when he himself was in the army, he was stationed for a time with an Ack-Ack unit in Bexhill-on-Sea on the coast of East Sussex. He described this rather quiet town as 'closing each evening at seven'. Spike is buried not far away, in Winchelsea, where I believe the inscription he wanted on his tombstone – 'I told you I was ill' – was at first not allowed. However, it is there now – in the Irish language.

How about some of those I haven't mentioned already; Julie Andrews, Jackie Collins, Claire Bloom, Eartha Kitt, Vanessa Redgrave, James Mason, Topol, Peter Ustinov, Bob Geldof, Michael Palin, Humphrey Littleton, Dave Brubeck, Larry Adler (complete with harmonica). Then there was Sam Wannamaker, on at least three occasions, while he was pursuing his heroic ambition to build the replica of Shakespeare's Globe Theatre on its original site on the banks of the River Thames.

Anthony Quinn had some rather salacious stories about his days in the 'Road' movies with Bob Hope and Bing Crosby, and the attention the two of them gave to the young ladies in the cast. Choices were made on the first day of rehearsals! More interesting, though, were the pictures in his book of some of his paintings. Quinn was a hugely talented painter.

Omar Sharif gave young ladies from all over Bush House an excuse to come to studio C23 with less than urgent messages, just to get a glimpse of him. I recall the superb moment when he makes his entry on the back of a camel in *Lawrence of Arabia*, in which he appeared with another guest, someone I had known very well during his early career in Bristol: Peter O'Toole. When Omar Sharif paid us that visit he was still living in an hotel in Paris where he spent much of his time playing bridge, at which he was rather good.

I think it is the unrehearsed and unexpected moments that make 'live' broadcasting such fun. I remember the day that splendid actor Sir Ian Mckellen was our studio guest. At one stage he said that he felt you could say things in the theatre that you could not say anywhere else. I quickly followed up with, 'Is that why you became an actor?' He paused for a moment and then, half laughing said,

'Not really. I became an actor because I am gay and I knew there were many gay people in the Theatre.'

I don't doubt there were more than a few people in Britain who already knew that he was a co-founder of the Gay Rights movement, Stonewell, though I didn't. Nor, I imagine, did most of our audience. You could say it was the most widespread international 'coming out' (or 'being out') statement that had ever been made.

Mckellen is one of our greatest actors, and I particularly enjoyed his film portrayal of Richard III. Set in the thirties, he is finally seen at Bosworth, seated in a modem jeep. So what on earth is he going to do when he gets to that great line as he faces his end in the battle: 'A horse, a horse! My kingdom for a horse.' It's brilliant, but I won't give it away if you haven't seen the film.

One of my most enjoyable interviews was with Alistair Cooke when he was quietly celebrating 50 years of his weekly radio broadcast, *Letter from America*. In spite of a huge number of requests, it was the only interview he agreed to give. Heather MacLean, our lovely World Service representative in New York, suggested it might help if I wrote a personal letter to Alistair, mentioning that I first met him many years ago when I was a correspondent for the BBC at the United Nations. Leaned on, I suspect rather heavily, by Heather, who also produced *Letter from America*, it did the trick. Before he could change his mind I was on my way to New York.

Alistair told me that his first contact with Americans was in 1917 when they eventually came 'over here', rather late in the day, to take part in the First World War. Some were stationed in Blackpool, where he was living, and a number were temporarily billeted on his family home. As a youngster he was fascinated by two things: their uniform caps so reminiscent of the Scouting movement and their ability to eat holding just a fork!

At the end of the Second World War a senior management figure in the BBC, Lindsey Wellington, came up with the idea of asking Cooke to do a weekly broadcast from the States, initially for a trial period of thirteen weeks. If it proved popular, it might be extended for another thirteen weeks. But in those days there were huge difficulties with sending money abroad for his fee. The value of the pound against the dollar was pretty poor. He was told: 'Don't be disheartened at twenty-six weeks if we say, "That's it."' The rest, as they say, is history. I particularly enjoyed Alistair's reflections on some of the American presidents. He thought both the Roosevelts, Teddy and Franklin D., were outstanding. He also greatly admired Johnson and the skilful, even devious, way he worked to get the Civil Rights Bill through Congress, leaning very heavily on some of the doubters, notably fellow southerners.

Like me, he also became an admirer of Harry S. Truman. He first saw a rather insignificant looking little man sitting next to him, enjoying a snack, at one of the rooms off the main hall where the Democrats were having their Convention. He was wearing what Alistair described as an electric blue suit and a huge bow tie. FDR was already enthroned once again as the Democrats' presidential choice.

When someone in the hall announced, 'Please welcome the next vice-President Harry S. Truman,' up got the small man in the electric blue suit and went into the hall, a little known formerly bankrupt haberdasher from Missouri. When FDR died and Truman took over there was a feeling of deep gloom and depression among the political leaders. That changed when they found themselves confronted by a very forceful figure, who often seemed to be rather better informed than many of them.

I suspect it may have been FDR who gave Alistair some inspiration for his long career as a broadcaster. Roosevelt was the first President to use Radio to speak directly to the American people.

The first of his 'fireside chats', as the broadcasts came to be called, was in March 1933. Catching the audience in their own homes one evening at the week-end, he used a 'quiet, confidential, man-of-the-people' technique that proved hugely effective, and never more so than when he was dismissing the arguments of the opposition. Leaning just that little bit closer to the microphone he would simply say, 'You and I know better than that.'

One other rather brief encounter I greatly enjoyed is available on a BBC LP, should you still have access to a gramophone. It is called 'This is London: 50 Years of Broadcasting to the World'. I assume it is still available to buy, although, by now, it could have been transferred to CD.

In April 1975 I briefly met the man who had recently retired as

Governor of California. Ronald Reagan was in London as part of a tour of Europe. There was just time to ask if he was preparing himself for an even more ambitious position? Would he like to be President one day?

'Well (chuckle) I don't know that anyone could turn it down if he were asked. But I don't know also of many instances where the people have gone out on a fox hunt for someone and brought him in.'

Was that a 'Yes'?

When Reagan became President there was much derisive comment about this mainly B-Movie actor occupying the White House as the leader of the Free World. Yet it now has to be accepted that his presidency was hugely successful in ending the Cold War and making the world a safer place. Certainly, Americans now regard him with huge affection.

One of the results of so many studio interviews I did over the years is that I now possess a splendid collection of books signed and presented to me by guests who were on tour for their publishers. One is from the first American in Space, later the commander of the Apollo 14 mission to the moon, Alan Sheppard. Another is from Terry Waite who just wrote: 'To John, with much gratitude'. I was particularly pleased with the author of a book called *Dateline Freedom: Revelations of an Unwilling Russian Exile*. I met Vitali Vitaliev just a year after he and his wife and son, had fled from Moscow into Poland. Even in the years of Perestroika, as the old Soviet Union was unravelling, he felt his role as an investigative reporter of the past was putting him in some danger. And what did he write in the cover of his book? 'To my favourite Radio presenter and first teacher of English.'

First teacher of English! I hope he wasn't listening on the day I interviewed Stanley Unwin, an old friend and colleague. It could have caused a severe set-back to his English studies. Stanley had created his own very amusing version of spoken English, which at times sounded almost like the real thing but not quite. As he spoke at some speed, and with some fluency, you were often left thinking that you almost understood what he was saying – and that if you didn't it was probably your fault. It was Stanley's mother who gave him the first word in his unique vocabulary. She came home one day rather bruised, having fallen over, or, as she put it, having 'fallolopped' in front of a tram.

I did the interview down the line to him in Northampton. This town in the Midlands is famous for producing footwear, or, as he put it 'in the Midloab for booty and shoey.'

Stanley used his great gift to some effect when he was driving around with reporters like me in one of the BBC's mobile recording cars. He liked to tell the story of the occasion when he was with a reporter, trying to get into an RAF base to send an urgent recording down the line to the BBC Newsroom. A rather stuffy gate-keeper refused to allow them in as they didn't have a valid pass. Stanley went into a high speed explanation which seemed to suggest they were on very important exercise that had already been approved.

The gate-keeper picked out enough words here and there that sounded authentic, whereupon there was a complete change of attitude. 'Why didn't you say that in the first place,' he said. 'Please come in.'

A few years after leaving the BBC, I opened *The Guardian* one morning and read something that made me very angry: 'World Service will not call US attacks terrorism.' At a Newsworld conference in Barcelona Mark Damazer, then the BBC's Deputy Director of News, based in Broadcasting House, was quoted as saying that the World Service would 'lose its reputation for impartiality' if it continued to use the word 'terrorism' in referring to the 9/11 attack on the twin towers in New York.

He went on to say: 'However appalling and disgusting it was, there will nevertheless be a constituency of our listeners who don't regard it as terrorism. Describing it as such could downgrade our status as an impartial and independent broadcaster.'

What nonsense, yet when I later bumped into two senior management figures, I was dismayed to discover they seemed to share Damazer's views. And when he moved on to become the Head of Radio 4, one of his peers described him as 'one of the BBC's leading intellectuals'!

I wondered what the most famous person ever to work for the External Services (as they were once called) would have said about it all. His name was Eric Arthur Blair. Born in India and at one time serving in Burma with the Indian Imperial Police, he spent two years in the early forties with the BBC in London and is better known as George Orwell author of *Nineteen Eighty-Four*.

Would he suspect that Winston Smith was no longer working at the Ministry of Truth but was now engaged in researching 'newspeak' at the BBC?

WAR IS PEACE
FREEDOM IS SLAVERY
IGNORANCE IS STRENGTH
TERRORISM IS HEROISM

Honesty and accuracy, telling it as we believe it to be – quite impartially – with no need to look over our shoulders, fearful in case we offend someone. Those are the standards of BBC World Service News and Current Affairs as I remember them.

I am sad to say that I would no longer want to work for the BBC. Ten years after I left in the autumn of 2007, I enjoyed a very happy evening with a huge number of old friends and colleagues who seemed to take the same view. We were all at a party in the Royal Institute of Architects in Portland Place to celebrate the 75th anniversary of World Service. Most of us were now retired, rejoicing in the good fortune of having worked in Bush House in the great days when it was universally recognised as the world's number one radio station.

There was one moment after my retirement, however, when I could not resist the chance to do another interview. It came when I was attending a memorial service for Frank Gillard. At a reception that followed I met the son of the man to whom Frank became very close as a BBC correspondent in the field during the last few years of the Second World War. His name was Lord David Montgomery, the son of Field Marshal Bernard Montgomery. I knew that David had for many years been a very close friend of Manfred Rommel, the son of Germany's 'Desert Fox', Field Marshal Erwin Rommel.

Unfortunately, Manfred was by this time getting increasingly disabled by Parkinson's disease and was rather confined to Stuttgart where, for twenty years, he was the city's enormously popular mayor. I asked David if I could take him to Stuttgart to see his old friend so that I could put them round a table for a chat.

139

David was more than willing. Like me both Manfred and David were about eleven years old (both were born in 1928) when the Second World War started in 1939. Neither David nor Manfred saw much of their fathers during the ensuing years. But it was Manfred who had to live through the most dramatic family crisis, a year before the War ended. In July 1944 Field Marshal Rommel was seriously wounded when an RAF plane spotted his car and strafed it. He went first to hospital and was then sent home to recuperate. It coincided with the attempt to remove Hitler with a bomb set off in his Head-quarters in East Prussia. There were casualties, but Hitler survived to inflict savage reprisals on all who were implicated.

Manfred's father knew nothing of the bomb plot, but his name was being canvassed as the person to take Hitler's place and to try to make peace with the Allies. Certainly the old 'Desert Fox', appalled by the terrible damage being inflicted on Germany by Allied Air raids, realised himself that the war was lost.

In the interview Manfred tells of the terrible morning when two generals came to their home, bearing an ultimatum. His father could stand trial for conspiracy or commit suicide and receive a state funeral, with assurances that his family would be kept safe. They brought with them a suicide pill that would kill within three seconds.

The Field Marshal's aide wanted him to stand trial because he was innocent. Instead, he chose suicide. So came the terrible moment when Manfred saw his father walk out of the house, knowing that he and his mother would never see him alive again. It seems he was no sooner out of sight of the house than he was dead, slumped in the back of the car that was taking him away. Official reports on Berlin Radio said that Field Marshal Rommel had died of the injuries he received in that attack on his car on an open road.

Had Rommel survived would two of the great military leaders of the second World War have enjoyed a friendship like their sons David and Manfred? David thought they would, and would have spent much time discussing military campaigns and tactics, and comparing notes. The two sons have long worked together on Anglo-German friendship and the development of Europe.

After the interview we decided to have lunch. Everywhere we went it was obvious that Manfred was a greatly loved figure in Stuttgart.

Everyone wanted to say how pleased they were to see him out and about. They were also fascinated to meet David, to whom they gave a warm welcome when they realised he was Monty's son.

I did not offer the interview to the BBC. I gave it to ABC in Australia where it was broadcast three times, twice in the week-end programme *The Europeans* and once more in ABC's External Service. To hear it in Britain you would have to pay a visit to the Imperial War Museum in London which was very keen to have a copy when I told them about it.

Looking back now over eighty years I have to confess again that luck has played a huge part in my life. Luck and, not least, good timing. I can first thank my parents for their good timing in bringing me into this world in 1928, ten years after the end of the First World War, and rendering me just too young to play any part in the Second. I even did my National Service in that brief, post war period before the conflicts that cost the lives of many National Servicemen in Malaya and Korea. I left Singapore just three months after the Communists launched their campaign to take over the whole peninsula, a plot of which we were blissfully unaware, even though we were made to carry rifles when we took the train from Singapore to Penang for that wonderful spell of leave.

I discovered how serious was the threat of a Communist takeover when I read an edition of Singapore's *Morning Tribune*, a copy of which I recently re-discovered in some old files. The large black headline on the front page was: 'Reds Hoped For Malaya Republic On August 3' and underneath: 'C-G Reveals Plans Which Went Astray'. In a broadcast, the Commissioner General, Malcolm MacDonald (the son of Ramsay MacDonald) said this:

Yesterday a Malaya-wide Red Republic was to have been proclaimed – according to a Communist plot hatched last March and which has resulted in the present wave of terrorism.

The Communist leaders decided to stage an armed insurrection. To introduce it they planned to promote widespread labour unrest, stimulated by their customary methods of intimidation: stabbing trades union leaders reluctant to join them, hurling hand-grenades and burning factories.

On May 1st they proposed to hold large and passionate political demonstrations in an attempt to impress the people of Malaya with their supposed strength. In these various activities they were frustrated by the firm attitude of the governments. Nevertheless, they adhered to the date they had set for violent outbreaks – early June – the idea being that a revolt should begin simultaneously in various parts of the Federation of Malay States. At some time during this process, not many weeks after the trouble began, they planned that it should spread to the island of Singapore. They expected that only a short time would be needed to subjugate the colony. Indeed, they had fixed the day by which the revolutionary tyranny on the mainland and the island would be so firmly established they could proclaim to the world the birth of the Communist Republic of Malaya. The date selected for this auspicious event was August 3rd, 1948.

The date of the paper, which I still have, is August 4th, 1948, the day before I and my RAF mates boarded the troopship *Devonshire* to return to 'Blighty' to be demobbed. Once again, excellent timing!

There is one other item on that front page that I enjoyed re-reading, the headline: 'Kremlin Talks Still Hush-Hush'. It is based on a Reuters report from New York: 'Although no report on the results of the Kremlin talks has been published, the American public is voicing cautious optimism over the possibility of an understanding in Europe. The fact that the three envoys returned to the United States Embassy in Moscow in cheerful mood after the three hour conference, is regarded as significant.' There was a time when I entertained vague thoughts of being a correspondent working out of Moscow. Somehow, though, I don't think I would ever have got on the air with a despatch drawing conclusions from the fact that three delegates had arrived back at their base in the American Embassy from those talks in the Kremlin 'in cheerful mood'.

Facts are what is needed – and a bit of back up perhaps from other sources. I have never forgotten what the great BBC Diplomatic correspondent Tom Barman said to me when I was working as his assistant. 'I will not mind,' he said, 'if you are not first. But I will be very upset if you are wrong.'

When I eventually made it to Moscow, many years later, for a special edition of *Outlook* I was rather thankful I had never been posted there. It was that miserable time of the year which was neither winter nor spring – freezing cold one moment and ankle deep in slush the next.

My ten years as a BBC correspondent in various parts of the world were between 1956 (New York) and 1966 (Vietnam). In my view the magic of the job has been almost destroyed by the extraordinary improvements (if you can call them that) in communication: satellite dishes, video-phones, lap-tops and all the other paraphernalia the modern foreign correspondent has to have within easy access, whether he or she is based in a country or sent out specially from London. With news programmes going out day and night around the clock, some presenter in a cosy London studio can now see someone thousands of miles away coming up on the screen to be asked that most persistent of all questions: 'What more can you tell us about this?'

I think I was extremely lucky to be a correspondent at a time when you could set off on your own on an assignment for perhaps several days, completely out of contact with home base, as, for example, on the two occasions when I was up in the Himalayas in 1962 and 1965. There were not many parts of the world at that time from which you could simply make contact on the telephone – certainly not in broadcast quality.

At several BBC bases overseas 'circuits' – an (allegedly) high quality line to London – were set up well in advance, on a regular basis, at the same time every week, though circuits could be cancelled if there was no-one to meet them or nothing of much consequence to report. To do that required a simple message, a cable, to 'Newscasts London'; that was the BBC's cable address. For the distant foreign correspondent, cables had, for a hundred or more years, been the main device for keeping in touch with head office. Composing them was an art in itself, bearing in mind that each word had to be paid for. Learning to create an entirely new vocabulary was essential, as in: 'Unupcoming circuitwise Tuesday.' One of the most famous and much quoted cables was the exchange that is supposed to have taken place between Evelyn Waugh, covering the war in Abyssinia for a London paper. Having heard no word from Waugh for some time, London sent him a cable saying simply 'Why unnews?' Waugh replied: 'Unnews is goodnews.' Extremely irritated, London cabled back: 'Unnews unjob.' The exchange ended permanently when Waugh replied: 'Upstick job arsewise.'

Is this an apochryphal story? Was it Waugh? It certainly sounds like him. It was well known that he could be rude and aggressive. But I salute him as the author of one of my favourite books, *Scoop*.

The Cable as an essential aid to communication has ... virtually disappeared, along with its domestic cousin, the telegram. How many families dreaded the sight of a telegraph boy getting off his bicycle and coming to knock on the front door during the First and Second World Wars, fearing he bore the news that a father or son had been killed in action? Telegrams were also sent on joyful occasions – to be read out at receptions after a wedding, for example. Pat and I still have a small boxful, dating from March 1955. Growing up in the thirties I can't remember that my family had a telephone. We did, eventually, in the late forties when we were living in Bristol, though I have the impression it was used more for receiving calls than making them.

Certainly in those days telegrams were still much in use. Like cables the economical use of words was essential to control the expense. I remember once listening to a radio programme bemoaning the fact that telegrams were no longer in service. One of the broadcasters praised their usefulness in economically alerting phoneless family members to the urgent need to make contact – 'Come at once. Mother sinking.'

At the age of eighty I can look back over my career as a journalist and broadcaster from the days of Pitman's shorthand and the upright typewriter to the sophisticated electronic equipment I am now using to write these memoirs.

Organising my own life has been absolutely at the centre of my long career as a broadcaster and journalist, certainly since I left the BBC staff in 1966. I have never employed an agent to find work for me or advise me what to do. For 34 years as a freelance I survived very happily in *Outlook* on contracts that were eventually renewed annually, with a reasonable increase and two weeks' paid holiday.

I retired when I wanted to as I reached seventy and am a very happy and financially secure pensioner. I am not sure how I have achieved that. Like my grandfather, who was woefully improvident and ultimately something of a burden to the family, I can never remember thinking with any anxiety about the future. I did, however, have some prudent financial advisors.

There is one delightful book in my collection that takes me back more than sixty years to my schooldays. It is an account of what life was like on the Home Front in World War Two. I never met the author as she was long dead. Her memoirs (in the form of diaries) were only discovered some years after she died. They were almost a day by day account of those war years, written in no fewer than fifteen school exercise books. I talked in the *Outlook* studio to the journalist, Peter Donnelly, who took on the job of editing them and finding a publisher.

Mrs Milburn's Diaries: An Englishwoman's Day to Day Reflections, 1939–1945 were published by Harrap in 1979. Clara Emily Milburn lived with her husband Jack and their son Alan in a spacious, detached house with a large garden at Balsall Common near Coventry. The family was upper middle class, prosperous and possessed no fewer than three cars: a Rover, a splendid old Morris coupé and an MG, the pride and joy of their son, a Second Lieutenant in the 7th Battalion of the Royal Warwickshire Regiment. They also had a maid called Kate who later stayed on with them to become a much-loved family friend. Alan was at Dunkirk and not among those miraculously rescued from the beaches. The Milburn's were uncertain what had happened to him. Was he dead or a POW? For some time they clung to the belief that he was a prisoner, though he may have been wounded.

This is the diary entry for Tuesday, June 11th 1940: 'A letter arrived today from Major Cox describing the action in which he thinks it likely Alan and his colleague Purchas [who was wounded] and 40 men were taken prisoner. A farmhouse where Maj. Cox and his men had taken up station could not be vacated for a moment because of 'murderous machine gun fire'.

Later, after a counter attack, Purchas, Alan and the men who had been placed earlier in a house 200 yards away were looked for. Nothing was seen of them at all, so it was concluded they had been taken prisoner.

In early July she is entering a note about Lord Woolton, the man she calls 'the forceful food controller', speaking on the wireless to announce that tea is to be rationed to 2oz per head per week and margarine and cooking fats are also to come under the rationing scheme. A week later she makes the most moving entry in her diary:

I looked in for a moment or two at the [Women's] Institute where the produce exhibition was being held to see how the judges were getting on and found them in the thick of things, tasting the merits of jams, jellies, chutneys, salad cream and bottled fruit. Mrs Ford was sipping each bottle of wine and looking flushed by the time she got to the eleventh!

About 5.30 I sauntered rather heavily off through the field at the back to take Twink [their small terrier dog] for his walk. When I was well away I heard Jack calling and saw him waving to me from the hedge. It can't be a telegram about Alan I thought, so I crammed that thought back and we met in the middle of the field. Kate has just had a telegram over the phone for us from the War Office. Alan is a prisoner of war. There and then saying 'thank God' we embraced each other for sheer joy at the good news. Oh how delighted we were to hear at last that he is alive and apparently unwounded.

Well, Twink and I went through the fields, and I came home to telegraph and telephone messages round to all the very kind friends who had so often inquired, or even shown their sympathy by their one expression and then their silence. Everybody has been so sweet and kind, it was almost too much to bear. Even the garage proprietor, Mr Cooper, said: 'We thought a lot of him'. After a very busy evening it is 11.30 and, with a heart full of thankfulness, I hope to sleep.

There is a lovely entry for Monday October 14th 1940, underlining the way society was brought together on the Home Front. Mrs Milburn has taken on the job of delivering what she calls 'Salvage papers' along her road. I think this must have been something to do with the request for old metal pots and pans, ostensibly to help build more weapons, like Spitfires and Hurricanes. Actually I believe we learned later that none of this metal was any use in the construction of aircraft. So I am fairly sure our old frying pan never got airborne. Anyway, this is how Mrs Milburn describes her mission: 'I found myself tremendously interested in my neighbours, both well-to-do and otherwise, and the great thing one learns is how very much nicer everyone is than one thought. Everybody's house is interesting and I got a smile and kindly words everywhere, and many inquiries about Alan and much sympathy.'

In the coming weeks and months of 1940 Mrs Milburn would be getting to know more and more people from every corner of society, and playing her part in offering help and comfort to evacuees and families whose homes were now piles of rubble. This was the height of the Blitz. On Tuesday, August 13th she writes: 'The Battle of Britain has begun in earnest.' The following day she tells us: 'Yesterday's "bag" of Nazi planes was 78 to 13 of ours.'

Night after night the air raid sirens, and the sound of bombs dropping not too far away, drove Mr and Mrs Milburn to the sanctuary of what they called 'the dug-out', in the days before they had a proper air raid shelter. Some nights were fairly peaceful and Alan's room was always available for complete strangers, who had been bombed out and were desperate for a bed and a comparatively quiet sleep.

The climax came on Friday November 15th with the raid that caused huge damage to the city of Coventry, with heavy loss of life and the destruction of the historic 14th century Cathedral. Mrs Milburn writes: 'After the blackout a woman called to ask if I could give a few nights rest and shelter to a Coventry couple who were worn and tired. I said yes at once.'

There is an especially delightful entry for November 15th 1940. Alderman Moseley, Mayor of Coventry, living in a small house in what she calls 'one of Coventry's lesser streets', had a distinguished visitor: 'His wife heard a knock and, as the bombing had upset the front door and it could not be opened, she called out 'Come round to the back'. The visitor came round. It was the King, who is going round bombed places!'

How wonderfully she evokes the indomitable spirit and feeling of comradeship that held people together on the Home Front during war years.

11

Les Idées sur L'Escalier

One of my French teachers told me that this is a delightful expression meaning 'second thoughts' or 'afterthoughts'. I quite often have *les idées sur l'escalier* these days – as, no doubt, do many others of my age. I have just locked the door and taken a few steps on my way out when I suddenly stop and wonder any of the following: Did I turn off the gas under that saucepan on the stove? Did I leave a tap on in the bathroom? Did I leave any lights on when I am supposed to be helping to save the planet? What did I do with that letter I want to post? And so on. Nothing for it but to turn round, go back in again and check.

And that is exactly what I am going to do with the final pages of these memoirs. What have I forgotten?

I have not yet mentioned a special edition of *Outlook* that helped us to sustain a reputation for being unpredictable. On July 4th 1976 we decided to do the whole programme as if it were 200 years earlier – July 4th 1776, the date of America's Declaration of Independence.

The main current affairs story of the day came, of course, from the other side of the Atlantic. The first interview was with the historian, Mervyn Jones, who joined us from the London School of Economics, opposite Bush House. He gave us a detailed account of the series of events that had led to this momentous climax; why the American Colonists had become so aggrieved and determined no longer to be governed and taxed from London. No taxation without representation.

I asked him if he thought there was any chance the Americans could win a war of independence. He thought it unlikely. A large British force was already lying off New York waiting to disembark from the British fleet.

Why did I for so long turn my back on domestic radio and television? I remember admitting to someone who was interviewing me for a magazine that it probably showed a terrible lack of ambition, or even my natural idleness. But if you have been reading these memoirs so far you will understand my feeling that I couldn't go anywhere that would offer more fun and more adventures all over the world than *Outlook*.

Nevertheless, Steve Bonarjee's warning that turning my back on domestic radio and television would lead to my being forgotten was partly confirmed in a very amusing way when I began what would be my last appearance on television. It was the first time I presented *Young Scientist of the Year*. On that Sunday evening when the first programme went out, one of our marvellous *Outlook* girls told her mother she wanted to see it. Knowing her daughter was not by nature a science enthusiast she wanted to know why. 'Because,' said her daughter, 'it is being presented by John Tidmarsh.'

After a brief pause her mother said, somewhat incredulously, 'Is he still alive?'

It was a TV production in Bristol of a play called *Yellow Sands* that introduced me to the man who, many years later, would become Britain's favourite Prime Minister, Jim Hacker (alias Paul Eddington). *Yes Minister* and *Yes, Prime Minister* will always be among my favourite television comedies. Paul was a great actor, with a marvellous capacity for expressing his thoughts in his facial expressions. *Yellow Sands* was his first appearance on television. Black and white in those days. Pat was actually in the same production and we sustained a friendship with Paul and his wife Tricia over many years, mainly through the exchange of Christmas cards. Not long before Paul died of skin cancer I managed to persuade him to be a guest on *Outlook*.

One person I would very much like to have known is the man who would have been my father-in-law, Group Captain Norman Pleasance.

The Group Captain died in March 1944 returning in a Lancaster bomber of 9 Bomber Squadron from a raid over Germany. As the Station Commander it was not part of his duties to join the aircrews on operations, though he had done it more than once before. The aircraft still had a bomb in the bomb bay, which the rules stipulated they should get rid of only in a specially designated area of the English Channel. They were just to the west of Brussels when a German fighter came up from below them, firing shots that hit the bomb and caused it to explode. The wreckage came down in farmland at a place called Lembeek, where there is now a small memorial plaque on the wall of one of the buildings recording the names of those who died. This has all been the work of someone who has become a very good friend of our family – Marcel Dubois. He has spent many years piecing together the story of the Lancaster and its crew after seeing an article in *TABS*, the 9 Bomber Squadron magazine, asking for any information about Group Captain Pleasance. That is how he came into contact with my wife Pat (née Pleasance).

Marcel's interest was first aroused when an aunt told him that one of the engines from the Lancaster landed in her garden. She thought it was an American bomber, but he said it could not have been as they were flying at night. The US Air Force did the daylight raids.

It was through Pat that he heard of the one surviver of the crash, George Caines.

We didn't know Marcel when we lived in Brussels. Nor did we know that the Group Captain and his crew are actually buried alongside each other in the City's main cemetery. We have since been there, of course, to pay our respects and twice to that field in Lembeek, where Marcel has in the past organised a brief event to recognise the anniversary of that day in 1944. Pat is now an associate member of the 9 Bomber Squadron Association and so is Marcel. The Squadron was actually formed in 1914 and Pat and I often go to the annual reunion of the Association in September at the Squadron's base at RAF Marham in Norfolk, where we now know two members of another crew who were on that same mission in 1944, 're-arranging' bits of Germany.

The 9 Bomber Squadron symbol is a bat and I am particularly fond of the Association's motto, created by re-arranging the letters in the word BATS:

THERE'S ALWAYS BLOODY SOMETHING!

In 2009 it was announced that the BBC World Service, both English and the languages, would be forced to move to Broadcasting House at the top of Regent Street, sharing the building with Domestic

Services, but remaining independent and still financed by the Foreign Office. It means that Bush House, for sixty years universally recognised as the world's number one radio station, will be abandoned. The building has never actually been owned by the BBC, although there had been an opportunity to take it over near the end of the twentieth century. The BBC and the Foreign Office put forward a plan to buy the building for, some reports have said, £30 million. The plan was blocked by anonymous officials in the Treasury who insisted it would not be a good investment. In the first decade of the twenty-first century Bush House was probably worth four times that amount.

Now followed these sad consequences. The lease, held by a Japanese company, expired finally in 2010. Time to go. The motto above the very impressive portico will no doubt remain as a reminder that it was an American called Irving T. Bush who gave the building its name back in the 'twenties, originally conceiving it as a trade centre and a monument to Anglo-American friendship. It says: 'Dedicated to the friendship of English speaking peoples'. Dear old, multilingual Bush House did so much more than that.

Index